Vampire Legends
in
Contemporary American Culture

VAMPIRE LEGENDS IN CONTEMPORARY AMERICAN CULTURE

What Becomes a Legend Most

William Patrick Day

THE UNIVERSITY PRESS OF KENTUCKY

Publication of this volume was made possible in part by a grant
from the National Endowment for the Humanities.

Editorial and Sales Offices: The University Press of Kentucky
663 South Limestone Street, Lexington, Kentucky 40508–4008

06 05 04 03 02   5 4 3 2 1

Library of Congress Cataloging-in-Publication Data

Day, William Patrick.
  Vampire legends in contemporary American culture : what becomes a
  legend most / William Patrick Day.
     p. cm.
  Includes bibliographical references and index.
  ISBN 0-8131-2242-2 (cloth : alk. paper)
  1. American fiction—20th century—History and criticism. 2. Vampires in literature.
3. Popular culture—United States—History—20th century. 4. Horror tales, American—
History and criticism. 5. Vampire films—History and criticism. I. Title.
PS374.V35 D39 2002
813'.509375—dc21
2002011001

This book is printed on acid-free recycled paper meeting
the requirements of the American National Standard
for Permanence in Paper for Printed Library Materials.

Manufactured in the United States of America.

CONTENTS

PREFACE

As with any story that exists primarily in the realm of commercial entertainment, taking vampire stories seriously is almost as risky as confronting the nosferatu in the crypt. The modern vampire, as opposed to his folklore ancestor, is a performer, and the cape, the evening clothes, even the fangs are at times vaguely silly, a fact acknowledged in such comic vampire movies as Mel Brooks's *Dracula: Dead and Loving It!* Among the mass of vampire stories to be used for thrills and forgotten are works created by writers, filmmakers, and television producers who, though confined by commercial entertainment, don't simply want to sell an evening with the vampire but to communicate in a serious way with a popular medium. The accumulated presence of the vampire story, versatile as well as pervasive, gives individual tales a thickness and weight. As writers respond to their own moment through a vampire story they enhance the vampire story's depth and breadth, making it increasingly flexible and sophisticated. The possibilities for meaning in the vampire story result not simply from the dense variety of its versions but also because no matter how deeply absorbed we might become, we always know that the vampire is one of our great marketable nightmares—at once serious and childish—that serves as part of our common language. To engage with the vampire as a writer, director, producer, actor, or audience is to consciously choose to enter this realm of fiction where we know meaning can be made rather than, as is the case with realism, appear to be found. To reject these stories because they are "mere entertainment" is in a sense to reject imagination itself, to turn away from the possibility that fictional narratives can offer us meaning.

In taking such vampire stories seriously we could say they are Mythic in the sense Carl Jung, Northrop Frye, and Joseph Campbell have used the term, that they are alive with a primal human reality that encodes the shape and meaning of our existence. Because of their folklore origin, vampire stories seem particularly good candidates for such Mythic status. But as commercial products, vampire stories circulate as a pastiche of myth, reminding us of the primal and eternal but simultaneously signifying their dissolution into entertainment. As commercial entertainment, vampire stories also seem barred from the status of Art. To say that vampire stories are not Art is not to say that vampire stories aren't artful, made by skilled and talented writers, directors, and actors. It does indicate that their status is quite different from the works we call Art; because of their commercial qualities, we recognize them as creations of the moment, claiming our attention in different ways than works we think of as timeless masterpieces.

Another way of approaching vampire stories is to say that as with any commodity—gasoline, pork bellies, microwaves, stocks and bonds—these stories are highly reactive to the market, providing a sensitive barometer of the social reality in which they exist. From this perspective, stories that circulate as commercial entertainment are typically regarded as unreflective and unmindful *things* that convey an inarticulate ideology without understanding it. To examine stories in this way is to explicate for the culture what it cannot discern in much the same way a psychoanalyst might explain the dreams of a resistant patient, a comparison echoing Horkheimer's comment that "popular culture is psychoanalysis in reverse." This approach, though, tends to assume that stories are a kind of synecdoche for culture rather than a part of it, that they are, like pork bellies or gasoline, fungible commodities that are not experienced individually, and even more problematically, it assumes that the critic is to some degree outside the culture they examine.

I take these vampires stories seriously as part of an ongoing conversation about who we are and what we're about, one which I have chosen to join. I accord to vampire stories the status of a serious, mindful response to our culture, a dialogue carried out through images and narratives, simply because if I don't assume this about them, I don't see how I can assume it about myself. Vampire stories are located on the uneasy ground between Art and commodity, at the meeting point of entertainment and rhetoric, neither myth nor masterpiece, but also not merely raw inarticulate cultural data or ideology's packhorse. Criticism, stories, and the parts of our lives we call culture are all elements of a larger whole, and it is unfortunate when we mistake the results produced by our analytical tools for a perspective outside that whole. I'm making the same kind of claim that anyone who writes serious vampire stories does: look at the vampire story in this way and see things about our world, ourselves, and our imaginations that would not have been otherwise apparent. In taking this approach, I recall one of my students saying, when he became infuriated at the idea that *Salem's Lot* might "mean" something, "you can't prove anything with vampires!" This is true, but I doubt one can prove anything with *any* imaginative creation. I don't intend to prove things about our imaginative and cultural life, I simply intend to take part in it.

My understanding of these stories is inevitably retrospective; seen through such a lens, the vampire story may appear to be "going" somewhere, but that is a bearing my own perspective creates. There is no teleology here—the seeds of *Buffy* were not lying dormant within *Dark Shadows,* nor was there an inevitable route from *Dracula, Prince of Darkness* to *Bram Stoker's Dracula.* There is not even a real dialectic; though I think these works are often created in response to each other, they move toward proliferation rather than synthesis. Only a literary critic would be equally interested in all vampire stories, and all the modes of the vampire story can coexist at the same moment for different, if occasionally overlapping, audiences. Though our conversation about who and what we are may follow both a track of internal logic and external influence, it is more incoherent and complex than that.

Given the overwhelming number of vampire stories in circulation today, the decisions I have made about which novels, movies, and television programs to discuss means my argument begins invisibly in this selection process. In the course of writing this book I have tried to include vampire stories I thought were important voices in our culture. But works such as *The Night Stalker, Blood for Dracula, 'Salem's Lot, Near Dark, Martin, Children of the Night, Forever Knight,* and *Buffy the Vampire Slayer,* which I found compelling and entertaining, which even now I return to with special pleasure, were what led me to begin exploring these stories. As I worked on this book, my admiration of Chelsea Quinn Yarbro's work grew tremendously, and I discovered Suzy McKee Charnas's extraordinary novel *The Vampire Tapestry* and Abel Ferrera's brilliant movie *The Addiction*. And all of this began with *Dark Shadows*, which I encountered one afternoon in 1967 when I had nothing else to do. As I enjoyed them, then worked to understand them, they helped create my reading of the vampire story, just as I have undoubtedly recreated them in writing about them.

Thus, although as a critic I must play the role of Van Helsing (he and, of course, Mina are my favorite characters in *Dracula*) in pursuing the vampire story, I don't chase after them simply to drive the stake of analysis through their hearts. The subject of this book is its argument, but the object of that argument is the unruly collection of texts that constitute the contemporary vampire story and from which this argument grew. Though writing in the genre of literary criticism necessitates taking on the role of mythographer, I haven't stepped out of the vampire story. The genre of criticism demands that I bring order to "the vampire story," but the works I'm dealing with demand to be seen in their own specificity; my argument becomes an attempt to mediate between these two demands. This is why what I write is "vampire criticism," not draining the life from the vampire story but becoming in my own way a part of that story, summoning the vampire from the grave once again to become a new version of itself.

I owe debts of gratitude to Robin Roberts, Sandy Zagarell, and Jeff Pence, each of whom read a version of this book and made perceptive and helpful comments that allowed me to see my own work much more clearly. Sue Elkevizth offered invaluable help in preparing the final version of the manuscript. I owe a special debt to Jan Cooper, who read several versions of this book with curiosity, a red pencil, and a shrewd critical eye.

INTRODUCTION

I f you put on evening clothes, a cape, and rubber fangs everyone will recognize you; they'll compliment you on how elegant, sexy, mysterious, and scary you are. You can do this because in the one hundred years since Bram Stoker published *Dracula,* the vampire and its stories have become a commonplace part of our culture. Vampires are among us in such a variety of ways (they've advertised plastic storage bags and sunglasses and taught little children to count) we hardly notice how odd it is to be so familiar with an anachronistic bogeyman made by gluing folklore to bits of history.

Vampires are one of a number of fictional characters, including angels and space aliens, whom we treat as if they were real. While far fewer people actually believe in vampires (that is, behave as if vampires really exist as opposed to casually saying they think so) than in angels or space aliens, clearly we find it exciting to pretend we do. Their status as not only the living dead but the unreal real has inspired several vampire encyclopedias and reference books mixing entries on fictional vampires and meditations on the meaning of the nosferatu with folklore, history, and sociology.[1]

Our fascination with the vampire is evident in the popularity of the role-playing game *Vampire: The Masquerade* and in the number of people who put on the costumes for parties, clubs, and raves in the loose network of Goth culture. Most of this play and dress-up is a matter of fashion and fantasy, with the participants fully aware that their vampire identity is a game; though some people go beyond play to drinking blood and joining vampire churches, or "havens." Ted Bundy once characterized himself by saying, "Sometimes I feel like a vampire," making the symbolic link between the fictional supernatural predator and one of the archetypal real-life monsters of the late twentieth century, the serial killer, as if the fiction would explain the fact.

I think that largely because everyone knows Dracula (far fewer know *Dracula*), we have a sense that the vampire tale has always been one of our central stories, but this is only partly true. The vampire of folklore does appear to be very ancient; the modern vampire story goes back to the publication of John Polidori's short story "The Vampyre" in 1819, and of course Dracula has been with us for slightly over a hundred years now. Despite this extensive history, vampire stories became notably pervasive and took on real cultural significance only in the last third of our century. During this time, over one thousand vampire movies and novels, not to mention short stories and television programs of both whole series and single episodes, have retold, revised, and renewed the vampire story.

The proliferation of the vampire story in our era is part of the proliferation of horror stories in general. This proliferation, though, has allowed the vampire story to become more varied and more directed at specific audiences than it was when all horror stories were confined within the tight space of genre fiction. While critics such as David Pirie[2] see this as horror becoming mainstream, which seems only partly true, it is also a sign of the transformation of the mainstream through the shifting of popular culture from a genuine mass culture to niche-marketed culture. In this fluid situation in which high art and popular entertainment meld, the realm of genre fiction established in the nineteenth century—science fiction, horror, detective stories, sentimental and gothic romance, and historical fiction—begins to cross boundaries with realism, experimental art, and other highbrow forms.

Along with proliferation came diversity. Vampires became the protagonists of their own stories; vampire slayers, who were the real object of attention in *Dracula,* were eclipsed, only to return in the late 1980s and 1990s. Though the Count has not yet relinquished his place as Boss Vampire, today we have good vampires, bad vampires, ambiguous vampires, lonely vampires, vampires who only drink cow blood; we also have reluctant vampire killers and vampires who kill other vampires. Vampires have become contemporary American figures unrelated to the Transylvanian prince; while some vampires still wear the cape and speak with the European accent, more and more often they are the homeboys and homegirls of American culture rather than immigrants. Increasingly, naturalistic explanations for the vampire are put forth: either they have some sort of strange blood condition or they are literally another species (rather than the Devil's supernatural minions).

New and old vampire stories now occupy a continuous imaginative present. Stoker's *Dracula* along with the film versions starring Bela Lugosi, Christopher Lee, Jack Palance, Louis Jordan, Klaus Kinski, and Frank Langella (the last four all in the 1970s) have become contemporaries of Anne Rice's Louis and Lestat; Chelsea Quinn Yarbro's Saint Germain, P.N. Elrod's Jack Fleming; Nancy Collins's Sonja Blue; Joss Whedon's Buffy and her enemies The Master, Mr. Trick, and Spike; Mel Brooks's *Dracula: Dead and Loving It!*; and black-and-white independent cinema vampires as in *Nadja* and *The Addiction. Dark Shadows,* the 1960s vampire soap opera, never dies, continuing in reruns on the SciFi Channel.[3]

My concern in this book is not with the popularity of masquerading as the vampire, whether playful or pathological, or with the vampire as floating icon, symbol, metaphor, or advertising gimmick but with the stories that perpetuate such phenomena, tales of both the vampire and the vampire slayer. [4] From Polidori on—in the first sixty years of the twentieth century under the name Dracula—the vampire story was essentially a tale of the dangerous, though charismatic, sexual predator. The vampire story was a minor version of the myth of the "dark side," a cautionary tale about the dangers of sex in a time when the social aspects of sexuality could not be disentangled from the personal, just as reproduction could not be separated from pleasure; but they were also about sex as Original Sin, and the surrender to desire as the loss of one's soul. Quaint as these Victorian ideas may sound to us today, we have no reason to assume that the writers and contemporaneous audiences of these stories did not take them seriously. This does not mean Victorian authors didn't take pleasure in playing with such beliefs, but that ultimately these values provided a secure framework not only for these stories but for the culture surrounding them. This Christian framework was not always overt as it is in *Dracula,* but it informed most of the vampire story's existence through the mid–twentieth century. Today, the vampire remains a figure of danger and menace; as an image and icon the vampire appears in opposition to humanity and the world of order and meaning we have created, threatening to change us utterly into something dark and deadly. For some, this is the attraction of the vampire, the promise of the transgressive, the subversive, even the revolutionary, while for others it is horrific.

Although the vampire itself represents these things, the vampire stories are about something quite different. While tales of the dark side and cautionary stories about sexuality remain, as we have gradually let go of the equation of sexuality with Original Sin, the vampire has become an ambiguous figure in a story about the nature of humanity at a time when we are no longer sure we know what human nature is. Does humanity lie in our ethical nature, our ability to control our desires and needs, or in the liberation and affirmation of those impulses? Of course, the question is so starkly fundamental that one can find it throughout our culture. What gives vampire stories their particular force and interest in dealing with it is their location at the intersection of the supernatural and the historical. Vampire stories invoke a supernatural realm that is only weakly bound by theology and religion, and this is one domain in which we can look for metaphors and narratives that will help us toward understanding humanity. Vampire stories are also part of history; they evoke the ancient past of folklore and the immediate past of the nineteenth century, and these histories define another domain through which we may explore who and what we are. Finally, as the vampire legend develops its own self-referential history in the late twentieth century, vampire stories become reflections on the ways we narrate our identity to ourselves.

Vampire stories, both tales of vampires and of slayers, are part of a struggle to define a popular humanism in a world in which our dominant frameworks of understanding, Christianity and science, tradition and progress, appear to have broken down. Even the most apparently transgressive, subversive, or revolutionary vampire is part of an attempt to define and affirm our humanity. Over the last thirty years, vampire stories have addressed the loss of secure frameworks about human nature, about our relation to the past and future, and perhaps most importantly, the centrality of ethical choices for our sense of ourselves, particularly around the issues of violence. This book is an inquiry into the complex ways the vampire story explores what it means to be human in America at the close of the twentieth century.

Introduction

The fundamental appeal of vampire stories, what catches our attention at even the mention of the undead, remains their lurid, extravagant, exotic sensationalism. The titles of the Hammer Studios vampire movies of the sixties say it unmistakably: *Taste the Blood of Dracula, Lust for a Vampire, Twins of Evil, Dracula Has Risen from the Grave.* The vampire story is a chance to walk on the night side, indulge in the perverse, the forbidden, the dangerous, the supernatural. Vampire stories are, in a literal sense, sensational: they viscerally excite us with primal, forbidden, terrifying images and scenes of flesh and blood, fangs and stakes, violence and death, which bypass thought and evoke pleasurable yet disturbing feelings. Summoning up the taboos against cannibalism and necrophilia, such moments produce shock and arouse the fundamental physiological response of the fight or flight reflex (which is the explanation one friend offers for why she always ends up under the seat at a vampire movie).

Vampire stories are also tales of sexual sensationalism, the bite that is the kiss, pain that is pleasure, death that is love. But a vampire's sexuality is most powerful when it appears as an ambiguous suggestion of what cannot otherwise be portrayed, however transparent this suggestion might be. When, as is the case today, the vampire's sexuality becomes explicit, when both vampires and their victim-lovers know and even seek out sexual encounters with each other, the vampire has become only one more image of sexuality in a culture increasingly open to the representation of all forms of sex. While contemporary vampire stories often portray the vampire as a charismatic sexual being and celebrate the creature's erotic and romantic qualities, this is no longer the great, powerful secret of the vampire as it was in the nineteenth century or the movies of Lugosi and Lee, but simply another fact about it.

Vampire stories don't rely simply on sensationalism to interest us, though. Particularly today, the vampire serves as our reflection; after all, when one stands next to Dracula and looks in the mirror one sees only oneself. When vampires talk, as they often do, about how different they are from us, we may actually hear our own human voice addressing us, wondering who we really are. The vampire, immortal and yet dead, beautiful but monstrous, calls up the question of what it means to be human—whether that word has special meaning or is simply a zoological category like canine, bovine, or feline. That impulse to see ourselves in the vampire is a sign of an uncertainty at this moment in human history, as it means we can no longer be sure about the line between the human and the monster.

What does the vampire offer us? In transcending death, time, and space, unbound by the laws of God, nature, or society, the vampire is a figure of freedom and the gratification of all desire, the ultimate affirmation of the individual and, in one line of contemporary stories, an image of true humanity. But other stories emphasize the price for this freedom, because the vampire is also inhuman, pathological and unnatural, an undead thing controlled and driven by its thirst, a parasitic species dependent on humans, for their blood is its life, their bodies its reproduction. Vampire stories implicitly ask us: Would I pay that price for such freedom, such pleasure? Would I trade the light for immortality? Would I become a killer to cheat death? Could this be who I am? Thus, although the vampire has great power, it is also a figure of pathos, an outsider, and this fusion of mastery and vulnerability invites our complex identification with it.

We don't just recognize ourselves in the vampire; the vampire story is also about the vampire slayer. From Stoker's *Dracula* to Joss Whedon's *Buffy the Vampire Slayer*, the vampire slayer is an ordinary human who learns to imagine the unimaginable and confront violence and death, rising above himself or herself; this heroic fantasy is the alternative to the vampire's absolute, if not often monstrous, freedom. The vampire slayers fight not only for their own lives but for others who might be the vampire's prey. What distinguishes the slayer from the vampire at the most essential level is that the slayer is willing to die. Two underlying questions face all vampire slayers: Why am I willing to die to defeat this monster? What is there for any human beyond freedom, beyond the self? The slayer's real task is to do what the vampire cannot in going beyond the instinct, beyond the desire to simply live at all costs.

If these are the qualities that attract us to the vampire story, what kinds of uses do we make of these tales, and why? In one sense, the vampire story is a tale of our future, of who we will become as we leave behind the traditions and inheritance of the past and their forms of humanity. The future is a troubled place for us, as our assumptions about progress and the possibilities of utopia, so potent earlier in this century, have fallen away. While fantastic new technology continues to transform our material life, we are increasingly unsure that this is not simply change, rather than Progress, bringing as many problems as it solves. In the rupture that isolates us from the past while facing an uncertain future, ours becomes the era of loneliness and secrets; conspiracy and apocalypse now appear as equally plausible versions of our future as progress and utopia. It hardly matters whether or not we are more lonely, more secretive, more conspiratorial than people in earlier generations or other societies, for we have shown that we imagine ourselves to be so and frame our inquires about who we are and how we are to live around these assumptions. The vampire story is always a tale of secrets, of things hidden, of plots and conspiracies; applied to our future it easily becomes a tale of the apocalypse that will erase our connections to the past.

Ours is the era of disenchantment, in which all forms of value, belief, and truth are subject to ceaseless interrogation. Emancipation from superstition brings freedom but such freedom has a corrosive side. Demystification becomes disenchantment when it casts doubt upon our ability to produce anything but an endless chain of demystification in which value is traded for mere fact. Disenchantment takes the form of restless disillusionment when our desire for magic, for the supernatural, for transcendent order and power is dismissed as mere childish atavism without being at all diminished. In a world that becomes, to quote F. Scott Fitzgerald, "material without being real," vampire stories momentarily return to us a realm of magic and supernaturalism filled with a romanticism about our nature and the possibilities of freedom and desire. That this world is actually a product of our own nostalgia and anxiety is inescapable, but this does not make our attachment to it any less real.

Ours is also the era of violence; we may or may not be more violent than earlier times, but our consciousness of violence on both a social and individual level is central to our sense of humanity. In the television series *Forever Knight*, the vampire La Croix exhorts his friend Nicholas, a vampire who would become human again, to instead "feel the animal in your veins." It is to this intimate experience of our violent, predatory, animal nature that the vampire recalls us—raw pleasure without ethics, without consciousness or conscience. Contemporary stories chart the movement from sexuality to violence as the central theme of the vampire legend, for the control of our predatory instincts, not our sexual ones, has become the central problem of humanity in search of itself in the late twentieth century.

Vampire Legends in Contemporary American Culture

In her book *Our Vampires, Ourselves,* Nina Auerbach argues that "vampires go where the power is," changing their shape and meaning when the politics of the culture changes.[5] For Auerbach power is most importantly manifest in the representations of gender and sexuality, which trace and follow the lines of political power in very direct ways. Her book is a complex attempt to reclaim the vampire story as part of a female tradition that embodies outlaw and forbidden sexuality and modes of gender—even if the vampire, as she says, is a "turncoat," a false revolutionary who in the end expresses the dominant cultural orthodoxy. I agree with Auerbach that, at least in the last forty years, the vampire has changed shape and meaning and that power, sexuality, and gender form a significant part of the vampire story. But the other side of power is ethics, and I think that the vampire story has responded even more sensitively and complexly to the search for an ethical understanding of human identity, which emphasizes not our place in the grip of power beyond our control but our desire for significant choices about who and what we are. I don't assign ethics to the status of power's cat's-paw in the same way that I don't see art as the hammer of ideology; to do so is to surrender, under the guise of knowledge, to hopelessness and fear.

In this exploration of the contemporary vampire story, Dracula remains a central figure, for (as fidelity to Bram Stoker's novel is rarely a concern for contemporary artists) through the retelling and reinventing of Dracula's story, we recreate and understand our relation to that nineteenth-century past from which the vampire came. The Dracula story has two modes: the romantic Draculas of the 1970s, which have their fruition in 1992 with *Bram Stoker's Dracula,* and the Dracula stories of the 1990s, which integrate Dracula into the whole range of contemporary vampire stories, perhaps at the price of making *Dracula* disappear. I address the fate of Dracula in the two sections called "The Dracula Variations."

In addition to these Dracula variations, the contemporary vampire story has three complex modes that interact with the others in unexpected ways. The first of these, the vampire protagonist, considered in the chapter "The Vampire Liberation Front," is not a supernatural monster or Stoker's Antichrist but a post-Christian image of humanity ready to be set free from the restraints and limitations of an outmoded and repressive past. The dark side becomes the realm of desire that leads to freedom and self-acceptance,

8

even the possibility of a utopian community. Though relegated to tales of the outsider, these vampires appear to us as the true image of ourselves.

The second mode of the vampire story, which we'll consider in the chapter "The Post-Human Vampire: 'We Are Animals,'" reflects a counter view of such liberation from the limits of the past, one in which freedom becomes chaos and desire becomes compulsion. Rather than being an image of our true humanity, the vampire is self-alienated and without center, a mere creature of its own needs. The post-human vampire is a threat no longer from the ancient past but of a future that bears down upon us.

The third mode of the vampire story is the slayer story. Such tales never disappeared entirely, but the slayer vanishes from vampire protagonist stories, while the post-human vampire stories portray either a slayerless world or one in which the slayer is ineffective. But the post-human vampire does offer an opponent for the slayer, whose stories are about going beyond both need and desire to a new heroism rooted in the affirmation of community and friendship. The chapter "The Return of the Slayer" examines the representation of these values in popular entertainment.

1

VAMPIRE HISTORY

Since this is a book about vampire stories at the end of the twentieth century rather than the meaning of older vampire stories for their original audiences, one might wonder why it is necessary to address the history of the vampire story at all. My argument is not that there is a kind of vampire story DNA manifested in continuous line of recombinant descent from the vampires of folklore to Buffy Summers's battles with the undead every Tuesday on *Buffy the Vampire Slayer*. The vampire is not a monolithic archetype repeated through the ages. In fact, the history of the vampire story has been quite discontinuous. Until recently there was little concern with the vampire story as a tradition among writers and even less among readers; thus there has been no accretion of significance that builds to our current bumper crop of vampire tales. But the very fact that we might expect a history as the basis for understanding contemporary vampire stories is virtually the answer to this issue, for it reflects our assumption that if something is meaningful in the present, part of that meaning lies in the past. History, as always, begins in the present and finally ends there as well.

We are now so conscious of the vampire story that it needs a past to be part of our present, a need that has motivated us to return to older stories to create a history for our own. Our current vampire stories provide the lens that allows us to see earlier stories as meaningful to us, and our awareness of these older tales in turn becomes part of the way in which we imagine the vampire legend. This impulse to know the vampire as part of history is evident in the amassing of vampire encyclopedias, the republication of older vampire stories, the circulation of older vampire movies, and in the sustained popularity of "history of the vampire" books throughout the last thirty years.[1] For this reason, contemporary vampire stories are often set in the past, which was not the practice in the nineteenth century. It is why we grapple with Stoker's *Dracula* through revising, rewriting, and retelling, when earlier in the century plays and movies were content to simply take the name and a few details, forgetting the novel itself.

The process of creating meaning in the present is in part imagining links to the past; it is as such a link, for instance, that *Dracula* has come to our attention again. Contemporary vampire stories now not only have a past but represent the past to us, both the world of folklore and myth and the romantic and Victorian heritage of the nineteenth century. Through our reconstructions of the vampire, explicit or implicit, as a romantic Byronic figure and as an image of Victorian moralism, we give structure to our own use of the vampire as a romantic transgressor and a protagonist in the struggle for freedom from repression. We find in the vampire an image of the history of gender and sexuality because these issues concern us today. I don't disagree with these reconstructions, as they seem to me rooted in facts about the earlier versions of the vampire story, but we have emphasized them because they enable us to see our vampires more clearly. Thus, although contemporary vampire stories are essentially tales of our future, they are also tales of our past, for to move into the future means recreating our relation to the past. Virtually all vampire stories now carry the burden of the past as part of their significance, a burden that reflects our conflicting responses of rebellion and nostalgia toward tradition.

The fact that the vampire, unlike Frankenstein's creature, has a folkloric existence outside popular fiction, though, has helped earn it its special status as the unreal real; even the most skeptical rationalists recognize that folklore is real, whatever they think of vampires. The vampire of European folklore primarily served to provide an explanation for the spread of fatal illness among a family or group of neighbors in an era in which the mechanisms of contagion were unknown. Thus, from the beginning, vampires were a metaphor, though people didn't realize it, giving human shape to viruses and bacteria. The vampires of folklore are diverse but were relatively circumscribed in their time, however deadly, operating locally and restricted by a wide variety of rules, more even than the ones Stoker introduced into popular culture, such as the inability to cross running water and the fear of garlic, the wild rose, and, of course, the cross. While vampire legends appear in India, China, and Tibet, the modern popular culture vampire has its folklore roots in Eastern Europe. The dissipation of vampire folklore in Western European countries is one reason why English writers borrowed a German word for the undead.[2]

The advent of vampire stories in modern popular culture has its roots both in the recovery of traditional folklore, which began in the eighteenth century, and, paradoxically, in the rise of scientific investigation of strange phenomenon. From the late seventeenth to the mid–eighteenth century, interest in reports of real vampires led to an inquiry into their existence in Germany that is sometimes called "The Great Vampire Debate." The men engaged in this debate, typically priests and professors, became, in effect, real-life vampire hunters, scientists testing whether the tales of the undead that circulated in the peasant culture had any substance.[3] They opened graves and found bodies that, seemingly undecayed, appeared to be vampires, though some argued that this was simply a matter of natural processes. Evidence of premature burial was also often cited to verify the existence of vampires.[4] Despite the fact that any serious scientific investigation of vampires was bound to reduce such reports to mere superstition, the debate and the reports of vampire attacks gave vampire tales a new life in urban middle-class culture. The vampire of folklore also enables one of the central tropes of vampire fiction, the "Stoker got his sources wrong" motif, used explicitly or implicitly, to introduce new elements into the vampire legend.

The contemporary vampire story gives us a perspective through which to examine the folklore, while the folklore paradoxically provides both an air of authenticity and an air of myth for the contemporary stories. Interest in the folklore of the vampire is also an expression of our increasing contemporary fascination with the supernatural. The scientific investigation of vampires has turned into the recovery of the historical Dracula (in the books by MacNally and Florescu) and the late-seventeenth-century "Blood Countess," Elizabeth Bathory, as well as the psychology and sociology surrounding such "real" vampires. Noreen Dresser's thoughtful *American Vampires* doesn't take the undead seriously but does explore the habits of people who drink blood and live as if they are vampires.[5]

Though vampires appear in Germany with the 1748 poem "Der Vampyre," followed by Goethe's "The Bride of Corinth" in 1797, the modern line of vampire stories is really inaugurated with John Polidori's short story "The Vampyre," published in 1819.[6] The process of assimilating folklore to popular culture meant moving from poetry to prose and adapting the vampire to plots, conventions, and genres with which people were already familiar. Polidori's Lord Ruthven is an aristocratic seducer; "The Vampyre" has its roots every bit as much in novels such as *Clarissa* as in the folklore of the undead. It was as a story of the dangerous, charismatic, often aristocratic seducer that the vampire story existed for most of its life. Polidori's story is clumsy at best but survived for many years as a footnote to the story of Byron and the Shelleys, for "The Vampyre" was Polidori's contribution to the competition at the Villa Diodati that led to *Frankenstein.*

When "The Vampyre" was published, many people assumed that Polidori, who was Byron's doctor, was simply lending his name to a story by his famous patient or alternately that Byron, one of the first modern celebrities, was the model for Ruthven.[7] (There was little that early-nineteenth-century readers wouldn't have believed about Byron, with some justification.) A general resemblance between Ruthven and the notorious poet certainly sparked much of the story's success, though by now few readers, particularly in the American population, will likely recognize the author of "Childe Harold" and "The Giaour" as an origin of the vampire. (This may change: Tom Holland's 1995 novel *Lord of the Dead* is about Byron as vampire. It was published in England, where they have a better recollection of Byron, under the title *The Vampyre.*[8]) Byronism is in fact one of the few pieces of the vampire story that might justly be called its DNA. While this link was kept alive in the history of romanticism rather than as an explicit vampire story tradition, it has made its way through Lugosi and Lee into the present as the vampire protagonist, the transgressive hero, beyond the rules and customs of middle-class society, beyond even Nature and God. The contemporary line of dark, brooding, and decadent vampires of a thousand vices and (maybe) one virtue—a roster of the mad, bad, and dangerous to know, the melancholy wanderers and tormented outcasts—extends from Barnabas Collins of *Dark Shadows* though Anne Rice's Lestat, Chelsea Quinn Yarbro's Saint-Germain, S.P. Somtow's Timmy Valentine, and *Forever Knight*'s Nick Knight and Lucian La Croix.

Despite the success of Polidori's story, vampires did not really catch on fast; from 1820 to 1960, sixty-five published vampire novels, mostly in English, though there are also German and French works. The vampire's existence in the nineteenth century is real but fitful, and insofar as it remained in our awareness it did so as a footnote to the larger, mainstream literary history. Keats's "Lamia" and Southy's *Thalabba the Destroyer* mix vampires with Orientalism, while Coleridge's "Christabel" is literally a fragmentary version of the vampire. Charlotte Bronte mentions vampires in *Jane Eyre,* but only in passing, as the "foul Germanic specters"; the vampire also appears in the poetry of Baudelaire and in Walter Pater's famous description of the Mona Lisa in *The Renaissance,* but these are not part of a larger narrative centered on the vampire; such uses of the vampire never became part of a major cultural theme and remained limited to the exotic, thrilling image or metaphor. [9]

While "The Vampyre" inspired popular theatrical versions, Polidori's most successful commercial successor was the long-running newspaper serial "Varney the Vampire," by James Malcom Rymer, published in England in the 1840s. Sir Francis Varney is a late Byronic figure with his own sense of honor even if he is one of the undead, a state he often laments. What is striking about "Varney the Vampire" is not simply its development of the Byronic vampire into a tale of pathos, but its reappearance in the early 1970s when the process of building the vampire tradition really began, after having been not only out of print but virtually unknown for decades; for some time it was not even clear who the author was. The Dover edition of *Varney the Vampire* was an antiquarian facsimile of the newspaper serial, over eight hundred double-columned pages in excruciatingly small type. In this read-until-you-go-blind edition, *Varney* became important because he had disappeared, filling in a gap between Polidori at the beginning of the nineteenth century and Le Fanu and Stoker at the end. [10] *Varney's* republication is a sign of the popularity of *Dark Shadows,* the vampire serial of the later twentieth century, and indicates the tentative stirrings of academic interest in horror and gothic literature.

While *Dracula* is clearly the most important vampire novel of both the nineteenth and twentieth centuries, the greatest vampire story of the nineteenth century is Sheridan Le Fanu's "Carmilla" (1871). A brilliantly written story, very scary and unsettling, the popularity of the vampire in the late twentieth century led to its recovery. While "Carmilla" follows the seducer story pattern set by Polidori, Le Fanu's gives us the victim Laura's first-person account of her encounter with Carmilla. This technique, which today we have learned to read as inescapably open to irony and ambiguity, gives the story a very modern quality. While she is frank in conveying that not everything about Carmilla pleased her and never expresses any desire to become a vampire upon learning that her friend is one, her final words have an eerie nostalgia about Carmilla—particularly as we know from the introduction that the author of the manuscript has since died. "It was long before the terror of recent events subsided; and to this hour the image of Carmilla returns to memory with ambiguous alternations—sometimes the playful, languid beautiful girl; sometimes the writhing fiend I saw in the ruined church; and often from a reverie I have started, fancying I heard the light step of Carmilla at the drawing-room door." The thinly veiled lesbian subtext within "Carmilla" is today less startling than Le Fanu's declining to overtly moralize the story. There is no question that Carmilla's love is deadly, but there is also no question that Laura is deeply attracted to her and that even the sight of "the writhing fiend" has not completely extinguished her feelings for the beautiful girl. Her shock that Carmilla is a vampire is re-markably dispassionate and her relief at having been saved, though real, is curiously muted.

Of course, in 1871 Le Fanu could count on an audience that would bring to the story the whole range of Victorian attitudes about sexuality and morality, but the story is striking even today for the frank exploration of how attraction and desire transcend not only conventional morality but our instinct for self-preservation. "Carmilla" first returned to public con-sciousness as the basis for movies that exploited a voyeuristic interest in lesbians, the cautionary tale transformed into a spectacle of sexual experi-mentation. Since then, it has slowly become one version of the female vam-pire story in response to the interests and concerns of contemporary feminism, often as a coded tale of repressed sexuality.

Bram Stoker's *Dracula* (1897) is a complex and ambitious work as well as a piece of lurid sensationalism that provided the name by which we know the vampire today.[11] By the 1990s it had become the classic vampire story, a status most honored not by reading the novel but by endless revis-ing. While we now think of *Dracula* as Stoker's Undead Express, flattening all other vampire stories in its path, for a long time *Dracula* the novel was far less important than Dracula the Count, who was in many ways simply a good, scary name with an artificial historical basis. Indeed, among the many reproductions of *Dracula,* it is not until the mid-1970s with Fred Saberhagen's *The Dracula Tape* (1975) that there is the slightest attempt to engage Stoker seriously. Dracula's durability certainly didn't lead to *Dracula* being taken seriously as literature until quite recently and then primarily as the involuntary twitching of cultural trends. *Dracula* has returned as a circulating novel because it has become the work against which new vampire stories, both revisions of Stoker's novel and vampire stories that have nothing to do with Dracula, can be written. Stoker's *Dracula* now serves as a synthesis of romantic, Victorian, and Christian values, ideals, and fears, allowing us to take it apart and create informing structures for our vampire stories.

The element of *Dracula* that has made it important for us today is that Stoker made the vampire a figure in the drama of history; in *Dracula,* the encounter with the vampire is also an encounter with the advent of modernity. The novel's human characters are aware of their own position on the edge of the new century, caught up with its technology, such as the phonograph and dictaphone, and the latest modes of medicine, such as psychiatry and transfusions. While Dracula is from a bygone feudal era and Van Helsing always emphasizes that Dracula is a primitive, he is also the first vampire to stake his claim to the future like a brilliant child. Unlike earlier vampires, Dracula is not concerned with even predatory intimacy but with power over nations; his predecessors brought death, but the Count brings the apocalypse. We recur to *Dracula* particularly in the 1990s because we too are our own fin de siècle, searching in Stoker for an earlier version of our own situation.

Dracula was one of about a dozen vampire novels published in the 1890s; it was not noted as anything remarkable, but was sustained by being put on the stage in a 1927 play by Hamilton Deane and John L. Balderston, which was commissioned by Florence Stoker, Bram Stoker's widow. Though extraordinary in their own right, F.W. Murnau's *Nosferatu* (1922) was also a version of *Dracula* (retitled after a tussle with Stoker's widow over the rights), and Carl Dryer's amazing, surreal *Vampyr* (1932),[12] essentially a home movie, was based loosely on stories by Le Fanu. Neither made any headway in displacing Stoker's Count.[13]

The presence of Dracula in twentieth-century culture was cemented by Universal Studios during the 1930s with Bela Lugosi's *Dracula,* [14] arguably the single most influential use of the Count, though it is an adaptation of the 1927 play rather than the novel. Despite the strong imprint of Lugosi's Count on our image of the vampire, the Hungarian actor only played vampires three times in his career, and Lugosi's *Dracula,* based as it was on the stage play, was already at one remove from Stoker when it appeared in 1931. The Universal *Dracula* and its successors were part of a group of horror films designed to generate cash flow for a financially strapped and generally mismanaged studio. Universal's Dracula, also played by John Carradine and Lon Chaney Jr., didn't stand out that forcefully from the other members of the monster group, which included the Wolfman, the Mummy, and Frankenstein's monster.

While the opening scenes of the movie in the Count's ruined castle and the final ones in Carfax Abbey are visually impressive, the sequences in London feel stage bound, including the now-campy bat-on-a-string effects. The Universal movie sets the story in contemporary times, though the scenes in Dracula's castle are from another world entirely, ancient, mysterious, and surreal; armadillos (?) scuttle about the crumbling, cobwebbed fortress. Though making the story contemporary is in line with Stoker, the 1931 setting lost the novel's sense of historical transition and much of its theology; the Browning/Lugosi *Dracula* is another cautionary tale of the charismatic seducer. It does retain, though, an important element of the novel by emphasizing the Count's supernatural qualities through his casting no reflection, the camera trick transforming him into a bat, and the strange exotic world of the castle, even if such elements are pushed to the margins by the deadly seduction motif. [15]

Though the quality of Lugosi's particular sensual appeal has faded since the early 1930s, there seems to be no question that he was regarded by audiences of the time as a tremendously sensual man who renewed the notion of the vampire as a romantic, almost erotic figure. Lugosi's Dracula is far more like Ruthven or Carmilla than Stoker's brutal feudal lord who takes what he wants. [16] The charisma of the movie star took the place of associations with Byron's celebrity. Even with his old-fashioned stagy acting style, Lugosi's portrayal can at moments override decades of parody, though it takes an act of conscious historical imagination to experience,

Dracula checks the luggage before his trip to England; Bela Lugosi in the 1933 Universal Studios *Dracula.*

rather than merely see, the movie today. Lugosi's *Dracula* is a strange relic of the early days of talking pictures. Even though it became a source for parody and an example of antique cinematic style, Lugosi's Count remains an oddly compelling character, probably still the first image to come to mind when we think of Dracula. But the fact is that Lugosi's Dracula became a strange relic of the early days of talking pictures. However, the parodies multiplied, including both *Love at First Bite* with George Hamilton essentially imitating Lugosi and *Dracula: Dead and Loving It!* with Leslie Nielsen as a truly befuddled Count.

The most interesting of the Universal movies is *Dracula's Daughter* (1936), which uses *Dracula* to retell "Carmilla," though Countess Dracula, played by Gloria Holden, is a deeply ethical person tormented by her father's legacy rather than Le Fanu's amoral killer/seducer. It's a fascinating movie that had no real context in the 1930s except as a suggestive tale of dangerous sexuality. The series aided in the Count's descent into parody by the mid-1940s (*Abbott and Costello Meet Frankenstein* is mostly about their encounter with Dracula who now has custody of the creature). Lugosi's own career collapsed, partly due to his drug addiction; everyone now knows how he practically died while skulking around his driveway for Ed Wood's *Plan 9 from Outer Space*.

For a long time, the Universal movies retained what vitality they had mostly as memories, as Universal rereleased *Dracula* only in 1947.[17] Then in 1958, as a part of Hollywood's battle with television, the Universal movies were sold in bundles to local stations as "Shock Theater," to be presented as late-night entertainment for teenagers. Universal encouraged the television stations to use exotic/comic hosts (such as Zacherley and Vampirella in Los Angeles and Ghoulardi, whom I grew up with in Cleveland, all of whom were parodied by *SCTV*'s Count Floyd character in the 1980s), which made it hard to take the movies seriously.[18] At this point, the vampire, though clearly a renewed cultural presence, was still only one figure in the horde of pop-culture monsters that included space aliens and mutant bugs, and not a particularly serious one. This status, however, would change when Britain's Hammer Studios and Christopher Lee made a Dracula for the midcentury.

The Hammer Films:
Dracula Has Risen from the Grave

Stoker's tale began its second major retelling in 1958 with Hammer Studios' *Dracula*, released in the United States as *Horror of Dracula*[19] to avoid conflict with Universal Studios. Hammer followed Universal Studios' 1930s practice by making monster pictures as a series, including not only *Dracula* but *Frankenstein* and *The Mummy* as well as other horror stories. The Hammer movies were occasionally decried by critics as depraved and more often condescended to as cheap, though perhaps enjoyable, pandering to a lowbrow audience. As with Universal, Hammer Studios was a frankly commercial enterprise.[20]

Producer Anthony Hinds, director Terence Fisher, and writer Jimmy Sangster, who were responsible for beginning the vampire series, were concerned with the craft of filmmaking, and Christopher Lee (Dracula) and Peter Cushing (Van Helsing) were serious actors, but their unified goal was to tell a story that would really earn the British censor's H (for Horror) rating. In order to accomplish this they had to think about how *Dracula* could be presented to attract contemporary audiences in both Britain and America. While shooting *Horror of Dracula,* Terence Fisher purposely did not read Stoker's novel, as he wanted the film to have its own internal logic based on the actors and the set design. Later, though, he said, "I think my greatest contribution to the Dracula myth was to bring out the underlying sexual elements in the story." [21] From the moment of its release, people realized that the true horror in *Horror of Dracula* is the Count's overwhelmingly violent sexuality and the chaos of desire he catalyzes.

Vampire stories have always been about the danger of sexuality, but in *Dracula* Stoker harnessed the sensationalist use of sexuality to his Christian moralism; when I read *Dracula* and then see a Hammer movie I'm convinced that Stoker meant his moral vision to be taken seriously in a way the Hammer filmmakers didn't. In Stoker's novel the lurid sensationalism and moralism are equally sincere, which is what gives the novel its power and why for contemporary readers it seems strangely obtuse about its own content. While the plots of the Hammer movies are, as with Stoker's novel, stories of deadly battle between Good and Evil, a second drama is enacted on the screen through images of the tension, rather than the confluence, between the moral story and the sexual spectacle. Even as Dracula is trying to take their souls, we see Lucy and Mina prepare themselves for him while lying in bed, accepting his advances as if he were a lover.

The power of the Hammer movies lies not simply in their covert exploitation of sexual images and suggestiveness but in the tension between these images and the overt moral, which reinforces our sense that what we are seeing is forbidden—risky as well as risqué. Indeed the actual scenes insist on this by suggesting far more than they show; at the moment of the bite, the cape swirls up, the screen goes black, and we are left to imagine the forbidden for ourselves. The most sexual and erotic moments occur when we are seeing a double entendre: the bite is the explicit sex scene we aren't allowed to view. The central effect of Hammer Studios pushing the limit of respectability was to involve the audience at a level that is more or less invisible to the characters—the drama of sexuality's representation.

What began as the Hammer movies' strength became a problem as the series progressed, though, as the edge of respectability continued to roll back. From backlit nightgowns, cleavage, and avidly sexual, if ambiguous, expressions, the movies advanced to bare breasts and the occasional butt (always the woman's) as well as thrashing and moaning. In the early 1970s, when *The Vampire Lovers, Lust for a Vampire,* and *Twins of Evil* revived Carmilla from her long sleep, [22] Hammer was openly pursuing something forbidden for their vampires to imply, moving away from heterosexual *Dracula* to lesbian "Carmilla." *The Vampire Lovers,* a straightforward retelling of "Carmilla," makes the most of the vampire-attack-as-lesbian-seduction aspect of the story, including a scene of Carmilla and Laura undressed for bed. *Lust for a Vampire,* the second Carmilla film, though ambitious, is incoherent; set in a girls' school in the 1830s, a "getting ready for bed in the dormitory" scene offers the opportunity for shots of half-naked young women and a lesbian student's ill-considered attempt to seduce Carmilla.

If the focus on the underlying sexuality was always clear, the exact shape of the cautionary tales was ambiguous from the beginning. *Horror of Dracula* streamlines the action of the novel to allow the story to be told in eighty-two minutes. Except for Van Helsing, the original names are all that's left of the novel's human characters. Jonathan Harker becomes Van Helsing's unlucky partner in vampire hunting and is turned by the Count early in the film; Van Helsing must stake him. Lucy is Arthur Holmwood's sister, and Holmwood is instead married to Mina, who is simply another of Dracula's victims. Dr. Seward is merely the family physician, while lucky Quincey Morris presumably remains safely back home in Texas. And while there is never a question that Dracula is evil, the only sign of religion is the cross Van Helsing improvises out of two candlesticks in the last battle with Dracula.

Christopher Lee, the Dracula of the 1960s.

The Hammer films implicitly begin to pose the question of who Dracula is in our time. Christopher Lee has said that he always thought of Dracula as a human being, even a heroic one. While overall Hammer's Dracula has more in common with Stoker's imperious and brutal Count than the earlier Universal version (in *Dracula, Prince of Darkness* (1966), the Count never even speaks but simply makes animal noises before attacking), in *Horror of Dracula* the Count is much more human because he is vulnerable. Although Dracula looks like an animal with his mouth smeared with blood in several instances, when he thinks Harker will be able to stake him before sunrise and when Van Helsing exposes him to the sunlight and his body begins to disintegrate, we see fear in his face. When Dracula's "bride" attacks Harker, a scene that is played as a seduction, Dracula races into the room like an outraged husband breaking in on a tryst rather than the novel's King of the Undead subduing his subjects. This Dracula actually has human motivations for pursing Lucy and Mina rather than mere bloodlust: after Harker stakes his companion, Dracula goes to Karlstadt (the story is set in Germanic eastern Europe, not England) to take Harker's fiancée, Lucy, in revenge.

The loss of the sense of supernatural and theological Evil—as opposed to the chaos of desire—is figured in both Van Helsing and the earthy Abbot Sandor, his substitute in *Dracula, Prince of Darkness*. As Hutchings points out, they are briskly professional, representing order rather than a spiritual principle of the kind that infuses Stoker's Christian heroes.[23] The script is also ambiguous about the nature of the vampire. While the cross is still anathema to Dracula and burns both Lucy and Mina when they are in his power, Peter Cushing's Van Helsing emphasizes a scientific approach to the vampire.[24] Van Helsing speaks of studying vampires as we do bats, likens vampirism to a contagion and addiction, and calls vampires "re-animated corpses." At one point he even refers to vampirism a cult, a theme elaborated in the non-Dracula Hammer movie *Kiss of the Vampire* (1964). Later Hammer films emphasized even more strongly the idea of Dracula as Satanist, "the most evil man in history." The appearance of these competing versions of the vampire, which are never resolved, suggests the ways not only Dracula but the vampire in general was being tentatively adapted to the post-Christian world of popular entertainment in the second half of the twentieth century.

As the series went on, the movies shed even their earlier, somewhat clinical version of the cosmic battle between Good and Evil (Order versus Chaos) in favor of a more sociological one. *Taste the Blood of Dracula* (1970) turns toward the conflict between two young lovers and the girl's repressive father. Not only does the father forbid their love and condemn his daughter's natural sexual desires, he's a hypocrite, a member of secret club that, under the cover of doing "charity work," satisfies perverse desires in a particularly degenerate house of prostitution in the East End run by an obviously homosexual pimp. During one corrupt romp they meet the aristocratic Satanist and degenerate Lord Courtney, who challenges them to sell their souls to Satan by drinking the blood of Dracula. The failure of the three hypocrites to drink the blood of the Master causes Courtney's death. The Count wreaks vengeance upon the men by taking control of their children. Even with the invoking of Satanism, the Count is actually a metaphor for the turmoil unleashed by the generational conflict in the 1960s and 70s: the sins of a self-righteous and hypocritical older generation are visited upon their children, who then destroy their parents while being destroyed by the monster the parents called forth. In the end, the movie is on its target audience's side; some of the young people survive to live and love in a paradoxically cleansed world.

A similar shift in perspective occurs in *Twins of Evil* (1971), Hammer's final "Carmilla" variation, which starred the Collinson sisters, *Playboy*'s first twin Playmates of the Month, as the evil twins (though one actually remains good). But *Twins of Evil* is almost campy ("Centerfolds of Evil") in its struggle to be erotic. The most significant aspect of *Twins of Evil* is the transformation of the rational, humane Van Helsing of *Horror of Dracula* into Peter Cushing's crazed vampire hunter Gustav Weil. The vampire hunter and his all-male allies, identified as Puritans, are every bit as frightening as the undead. Weil's anti-vampire crusade is clearly driven by his own repressed, sadistic sexuality, and the movie obviously figures repression as a sexual obsession that is the true twin of vampirism's unbound sexual violence. Weil is, of course, both so extreme and so antique that he serves as an image of excess rather than as an indictment of all forms of repression and self-control.

Finally, with of the general collapse of censorship in films during the 1960s, even realistic movies soon exceeded what Hammer vampire movies could do with metaphor and suggestion. The vampire's bite might *imply* oral sex, but when Luke Martin can be shown (in a discrete and "tasteful" way) performing oral sex on Sally Hyde in *Coming Home* (1978), the vampire's greatest erotic force as metaphor is no longer needed. The world of horror films changed too; George Romero's scenes of zombie cannibalism in *Night of the Living Dead* (1971) went far beyond anything Hammer was willing to do in the realm of violence, but even more radically, the film captured a mood of contemporary paranoia. While Jean Rollins's French vampire movies, such as *Shiver of the Vampire* (1971), were more frankly sexual than the Hammer movies, the increasing availability of more or less well-budgeted pornographic movies (including vampire pornography such as *Count Erotica, Vampire* (1970) and *Bite Me, Darling* (1972)) made Hammer sexual innuendo seem timid. Needless to say, the Europeans were far ahead of the British and Americans in exploring the pornographic and erotic possibilities of vampire stories.

Hammer always treated their vampire movies as stories of the Victorian age; indeed the strategy of double entendre is a version of a Victorian approach to sexuality. Hammer's *Dracula* and "Carmilla" series were both a recollection of and a rebellion against Victorian heritage conducted literally and thematically in Victorian dress. Victorianism here was not just the actual past but the British censor's office, which enforced a version of Victorian moralism upon the filmmakers. In effect, the Hammer movies worked in two different frames of reference—a contemporary Victorianism in which vampires are Evil and a more modern one in which they begin to develop the theme that evil exists in the repression of natural human desires and instincts. In using the trapping of nineteenth-century cautionary melodrama to appeal to mid-twentieth-century audiences, Hammer movies began to develop the possibility that the sexual chaos embodied in Dracula is actually the monster of Victorian repression.

From Caution to Initiation to Erotica

In the wake of the Hammer movies, more and more vampire stories appeared that, stripped of the moral perspective inherited from Stoker, frankly presented the spectacle of forbidden sexuality as the center of interest. Such stories are direct outgrowths of the sexual revolution and the increasing openness about all forms of sexuality in our culture. *Daughter of Darkness* (1971), based on both "Carmilla" and the story of Countess Elizabeth Bathory, the real-life "Blood Countess" of the late seventeenth century, exemplifies this cinematic world of erotic chaos and desire with the vampire at its center. This chaotic and mysterious sexuality portrayed in the movie is frightening but exciting, and it appeals to our erotic curiosity. *Daughter of Darkness* isn't exactly a cautionary tale, for Countess Bathory is barely more evil than the husband of the woman she pursues, a vicious sadist who beats his wife. Rather, it seems a downbeat view of all human sexuality, a story in which all sentimental and romantic ideas about sex are stripped away in revealing its links to danger, sadomasochism, and violence— fascinating, if exotic and scary, revelations of the wild side of sexuality.

It's difficult to talk about the representation of sexuality in vampire movies in a single framework of social assumptions. Changes in attitudes toward sexuality occur unevenly throughout American culture during this period, so while homosexuality is far from the closeted shame it was in the early 1960s, there is still considerable demonizing of the lifestyle as evil. The vampire story representations of sexuality are probably best understood as transitional tales in which older frameworks of judgment coexist with more contemporary ones.

At the same time, the vampire as the menacing seducer in a cautionary tale of sexuality never disappears, though in contemporary versions of this story sex isn't Original Sin but a personal and psychological issue, a matter of our relation to ourselves and others rather than to God. Because of our contemporary tendency to place sexuality in a psychological rather than strictly moral realm, facing the dangers of the outer reaches of sexuality are now part of its full experience; even if in the end we return to traditional values of love, romance, domesticity, and monogamy, such exploration is a necessary part of the process of self-discovery. Cautionary tales thus become initiatory tales asserting the necessity of exploring the fearful unknown rather than affirming nineteenth-century morals and controlling our baser impulses. In this sense, the initiation story is a liberating one, for it ends with its protagonists free from fear and able to act out their own sexuality.

Initiation vampire stories crossbred with the teen movie of the mid-1980s, often producing more or less playful erotic fantasies such as *Once*

Bitten (1985), in which the vampire is older woman (both in the sense of being played by an older actress, Lauren Hutton, and in being about three hundred years old), and *Vamp* (1986), about three college students trapped in a vampire nightclub by a truly monstrous Grace Jones.[25] *Fright Night* (1986) [26] is the best of these teenage initiation stories, for it expands the motif of initiation beyond simply sex to adult masculinity. Charley Brewster and his girlfriend Amy can't summon up the courage to actually have sex; then the handsome Jerry Dandridge, played by Chris Sarandon, moves in next door to Charley. Charley notices him dumping a body and calls the police; of course no one will believe Charley when he insists his sophisticated new neighbor is a vampire. Dandridge is a sexually dynamic and brutal Byronic monster[27] who represents every young man's nightmare, the combined terror of nascent adulthood and his own sexual inexperience. Deeply buried in the battle between Charley and the vampire is an implication that his undead neighbor is bisexual (he lives with a handsome human male protector and turns one of Charley's young male friends). But male homosexuality, as opposed to lesbianism, even after Anne Rice's novels, is still a touchy motif for more mainstream vampire stories.

Jerry not only threatens Charley but begins to pursue Amy. The resolution of sexual anxiety becomes folded into the quest to stop the killer; protecting himself and Amy becomes Charley's way of finding his own maturity and authority. The movie integrates with Charley's story a subplot about the aging host of a television horror show, Peter Vincent, played by Roddy McDowell, who Charley desperately assumes is a real vampire slayer or at least knows real vampire lore. Though terrified by the notion of facing an actual vampire, Peter summons up the resources to become the Van Helsing he has pretended to be and help Charley stake the vampire. With the Peter Vincent subplot, the movie becomes a tale of not just of adolescence but of men who are not conventionally masculine or powerful facing and defeating the charismatic vampire—though not until Jerry has temporarily turned Amy, who becomes a slavering beast in a low-cut dress pursuing Charley with dripping fangs. Amy is soon returned to humanity, but her transformation dramatizes a young man's anxiety about female sexuality. [28] The movie ends with Charley and Amy finally having sex, though we hear the hysterical laugh of the teenage vampire who has survived Jerry's staking.

The highly successful *The Lost Boys* (1987), [29] though a visually energetic film, never takes its story particularly seriously, becoming less an initiation story than a self-parodying tale about the duplicity of the icons of popular culture. Though *The Lost Boys* has scary moments and evokes some of the confusion and complexity of adolescence, it's always arch, playing the story for either laughs or visual effect in the style of music videos. The movie finally subsumes the vampire story and, with its mixture of the serious and absurd, the sensational and the conventional (all presented in an extravagant visual style), becomes fused with the youth culture it seems to approach with a critical edge, offering the same kind of excitement and stimulation even while cautioning against this superficial world by making it the vampire's domain.

The central theme of *The Lost Boys,* organized around loose allusions to *Peter Pan,* is the tension between the family, represented by the Emersons—two boys, Michael and Sam, their mother Lucy, and their grandfather, with whom they have come to live—and the world of contemporary adolescence, represented by the nighttime boardwalk and carnival culture of the beach town Santa Rosa. While the Emersons are a messy but essentially good family, their home of Santa Rosa, though somewhat idyllic, suggests the chaotic quality of contemporary adolescent life, a world of endless stimulation and the promise of excitement and freedom. Michael becomes a vampire because of his attraction to both a young woman, Star, and the gang of "lost boys" who, unbeknownst to Michael, are vampires. As Michael drinks what he thinks is wine with them, he is involuntarily transformed; yet, since he wants to join this gang who seem so independent and self-sufficient, this metamorphosis is implicitly what he desires. The drinking scene evokes a metaphoric link between the vampires and drug and alcohol addiction, as well as yet another buried motif of homosexuality. Since Michael hasn't drunk blood on his own yet (nor have Star or Laddie, a child the lost boys have also turned), he and the others can become human again if he and Sam find and stake the master vampire.

The master vampire turns out to be the apparently fatherly video store owner, Max, who is dating Lucy to make her a vampire mother for his vampire boys. The irony of the story lies in the fact that the apparently free and independent lost boys are in fact dominated by their "father," a very traditional family values nosferatu, though this irony does not extend very far beyond a plot twist in which the nighttime world of Santa Rosa is stripped of both its menace and promise. The film ends with a spectacular battle between the vampires and the humans, including the comic Frog brothers, two pre-adolescent would-be Van Helsings who have gotten their vampire hunting lore from comic books.

By the 1990s, in the wake of AIDS and a general reaction against sexual excess, the caution in these stories becomes more forceful. *Def by Temptation* (1990),[30] set in an African American community, links the temptations of the vampire (here literally named Temptation) with the dangers of life on the street, especially drugs and AIDS. The central character, Joel, is finally saved because he recalls the Christian upbringing he received from his grandmother. *Embrace of the Vampire* (1996) is about a young woman's sexual awakening through a seductive vampire. While *Embrace* includes an interrupted lesbian seduction scene that makes an abashed appeal to voyeurism, it also affirms the essential erotic and romantic appeal of the vampire while at the same time insisting on love, restraint, and a woman's authority over her own desires.

The cautionary tradition not only continues in the vampire movie but in realistic films as well. *Fatal Attraction* with its equation of sex and death, and *Basic Instinct,* with its lesbian subplot and S and M sexuality, are in effect vampire movies made into thrillers. Overtly about men's sexual fantasies and fears and the dismal fate of romance, both are moralistic sensationalism with a strain of misogyny that seems much bleaker than the vampire movie, in which the danger can finally be staked. Indeed, with their affirmations of romance, vampire movies such as *Embrace of the Vampire* and *Subspecies* are less terrifying than *Basic Instinct*'s supposition of the inescapably violent core of human desire.

The initiation story is the twin of the kind of vampire erotica we find in Poppy Z. Brite's anthology *Love in Vein,* "a shameless celebration of unspeakable intimacies" as it says on the cover.[31] In her introduction, Brite writes: "The vampire is a subversive creature in every way, and I think this accounts for much of his appeal. In an age when moralists use the fact that sex is dangerous to 'prove' that sex is bad, the vampire points out that sex has always been dangerous."[32] The "erotic truth" of all these stories is ultimately that danger is what makes sex sexy and that the further one can go in accepting that danger, the deeper one goes into the heart of one's sexuality. At the same time the crucial erotic moment is the acceptance of the ultimate danger in the vampire's embrace, and after that, the danger either falls away or consumes the character who has embarked on this sexual adventure.

In erotic vampire tales, the vampire becomes the bearer of the secret ecstatic experience of sexuality as a route to a transcendence and realization that repression had forbidden; it is in imagining the possibility of such transcendence that vampire erotica has its greatest power. Indeed, as vampire erotica is by definition about the sexual experience we can never have, the vampire's sexuality lies in what it suggests, not what it is. Both the initiation stories in which the protagonists draw back from the vampire at the last moment and the erotic stories in which they proceed affirm the erotic appeal of danger rather than the danger of the erotic. But both use the vampire as the boundary, the marker that defines the point of liberation from the fear and terror generated by ignorance or outdated notions of sexuality.

2

THE VAMPIRE
LIBERATION FRONT

The central event in vampire stories over the last thirty years is the vampire's transformation from monster or object of covert fascination into a protagonist embodying our utopian aspirations to freedom, self-acceptance, self-expression, and community outside the restrictions and limitations of conventional middle-class American society. Vampire protagonists are complex figures, though, varying widely in the nature and degree of their liberation from both social repression and the traditional characterization of the vampire as an evil monster. As with Barnabas Collins of *Dark Shadows,* the vampire is the part of us we must transcend, while in portrayals such as Anne Rice's Louis and Lestat, the vampire stands for our tormented, divided nature, dramatizing our struggle to become truly free by embracing our dark side. On the other hand, Chelsea Quinn Yarbro's Saint-Germain is an idealized figure with hardly any of the traditional associations of the vampire with evil, yet he remains forever an outsider.

The vampire protagonists are in part creatures of the sexual revolution's quest to emancipate us from repression. All that was necessary to change the fascinating sexualized vampire of the Hammer films from a symbol of unnatural corruption to a figure of repressed natural desire was the removal of the moralism that cautioned us against our attraction to them. When the vampire's liberation stops with the liberation of sexuality, we have the erotic vampire story; but it is virtually axiomatic that any vampire protagonist is a figure not only of sexual freedom but of transcendent individuality. Since Freud, we have been tantalized by the idea that sexuality is the central, even defining quality of identity, and in the vampire protagonist the liberation of sexual desire becomes an emblem of the fullest experience of the self. The vampire protagonist is not simply a figure of sexual freedom but of artistic sensibility, wisdom, and insight—not just liberated desire but the apotheosis of the human.

Thus, the vampire protagonist embodies the aspirations to psychological and spiritual freedom that are the basis of such self-help psychologies such as The Human Potential Movement and various forms of New Age religion, which offer alternatives to the apparent rigidity and conservatism of Christianity. These dreams of liberation, which in their most utopian form reject even the idea of the dark side as nineteenth-century delusion, assert that the true fulfillment of humanity results when all aspects of our identity become liberated from the various forms of repression dominating middle-class society. Through acceptance of our inner vampire, we become at one with ourselves, and the deadly dualities of vampire/human, day/night, sacred/profane, life/death, good/evil become unified. Sexual, stylish, and supernatural, the vampire almost seems to have been imagined expressly to fill such a role.

Even as vampires became images of personal freedom and individual transcendence, the desire for community, for a sense of belonging, is equally acute in these stories. In the wake of the upheaval and change that travel under the generic name of the Sixties, America and its institutions seemed less and less able to sustain traditional forms of family and society, but the American desire for an ideal, utopian community remained strong, and this impulse is powerfully present, if sometimes buried, in stories of the vampire protagonist. Just as stories about sexual liberation are rooted in the sexual revolution, tales of the vampire in search of community have a tangential relation to the political and social liberation movements of this era, particularly feminism and gay rights, whose emphasis on issues of gender and sexuality were easily meshed with the vampire story. While transforming the vampire into an image of humanity is in a sense a gesture of rebellion, since as an outsider the vampire protagonist appears to reject all forms of traditional values, at heart these vampires aspire to love, family, and community far more than revolution. They are, in the end, alienated rather than radical and, in many instances, truer to the purported ideals of conventional society than the humans around them. Stories of the vampire protagonist are typically not political in a programmatic sense even if they offer apparently revolutionary versions of human identity. These are stories of the liberation of our desires, the drama of the self, and the generalized ideal of a community in which the individual is accepted for whatever she or he is.

Even as the protagonist, the vampire remains an outlaw and outsider, a fugitive with a dark secret. Vampire protagonists are part of the American idealization of such characters, which became particularly intense in the late 1960s and the 1970s when our relation to traditional forms of American culture and figures of authority became particularly antagonistic. The story of the vampire protagonist has such appeal because of an unsolvable problem at its center. The vampire may present an image of the human, but their power comes from the fact that they are not human. They are by classification outsiders, if not outlaws and fugitives, so the story of the vampire protagonist is typically a story of the struggle to find an elusive freedom, self-acceptance, and community. But even when vampire protagonists are unable to overcome torment and achieve full liberation, they live a deeper, fuller, more truly human existence.

The creation of the vampire protagonist begins with a daytime television series, *Dark Shadows* (1966–71), and two novels by Anne Rice, *Interview with the Vampire* (1975) and its successor, *The Vampire Lestat* (1985). Like the Hammer Dracula films, these tales recreate the past—particularly the nineteenth century—as the scene of their drama, but each endows the undead with a psychological complexity that, unequivocally changing the vampire from an "it" into a "him" or a "her," infuses the vampire story with a thoroughly contemporary sensibility. The great revelation in *Dark Shadows* is that the vampire has his own story, while Rice's insight is that we want to hear that story from his own lips, because that story is ours.

"Bite me, Barnabas"

If one moment is the locus of the vampire story's beginning as a significant contemporary tale, it is April 18th, 1967, when Barnabas Collins, the "reluctant vampire," appeared in the 211th episode of *Dark Shadows*.[1] The daytime series, which began as a conventional gothic romance with a governess in a mysterious mansion, was in danger of cancellation before it "went supernatural," as director Lela Swift phrased it; the appearance of Barnabas saved the show. Barnabas's popularity was extraordinary; Jonathan Frid, who played the character, received literally thousands of romantic letters, including one accompanied by a picture of the sender, naked to the waist, with "Bite me, Barnabas" written on it.

Dark Shadows helped create the contemporary audience for the vampire story by presenting it on television, the dominant narrative medium of late-twentieth-century America, not as a relic from the days of black-and-white movies but as a contemporary tale. The *Dark Shadows* version of the vampire resulted from an essentially accidental form of niche marketing; broadcast at 4 p.m. weekdays, the show's audience consisted of a demographic cross section of housewives and students. The former responded to the romantic aspects of the vampire, while the latter were captivated by the mystery of Barnabas, a man who was also a dangerous creature of the night, and caught up in a sense that they were seeing something daring. When I attended college, I found a group of students who met every afternoon in the student union to watch the program.

Though in retrospect *Dark Shadows* hardly seems to qualify for revolutionary status, the cast and producers always recognized that within the context of daytime television they were doing something radical, as did the audience. Producer Dan Curtis, series creator Art Wallace, writers Gordon Russell and Sam Hall, and director Lela Swift's merging of daytime drama with the vampire legend created a hybrid that was as unique for television as it was for vampire stories at that time. While daytime dramas always focused on the emotional lives of characters, they had not yet dealt with the bizarre, violent, and supernatural, nor had they portrayed characters with such obvious symbolic resonance. It was not merely Barnabas who appealed to the viewers as something new and exciting, rather the vampire story itself became associated with the daring and experimental.

As a television series, *Dark Shadows* is an unfolding text that transformed itself as long as it continued, becoming something new at each point in its existence; this unfolding quality characterizes the treatment of the vampire in the series. Rewriting the vampire as the protagonist of the story began cautiously, as Barnabas Collins initially appeared as the great secret danger to the inhabits of "The Great House at Collinwood" and the

Barnabas Collins, Vampire; Jonathan Frid in the television series *Dark Shadows.*

people of Collinsport. Barnabas was originally intended to be a traditional evil vampire who would be staked after a few months of thrills and peril for the human characters. The early Barnabas was always on the verge of violence. Cruel, domineering, and obsessive, he perpetuated such crimes as kidnapping Maggie Evans, a young woman from Collinsport, and trying to transform her into his long-dead beloved, Josette. What changed him was the response of the audience to his appearance in the drama.

The overwhelmingly positive viewer reaction to Barnabas led to a gradual change in focus as Curtis and the others realized that the vampire was becoming their central character.[2] Inspired by a typo in an early script treatment, Dr. Julian Hoffman, intended as the series' Van Helsing, became Dr. Julia Hoffman. By her account, Grayson Hall began playing her own conception of Hoffman as a slightly mad scientist not simply trying to treat Barnabas's vampirism as a blood disorder but falling in love with him, which got even more positive audience reaction. Finally accepting that Barnabas was now the central character, the producers killed off Dr. Dave Woodard, their second attempt to create a vampire slayer.

Once it was decided that Barnabas would fill the role of protagonist, the writers went back to 1795 to tell how Barnabas became a vampire under the spell of Angelique, a witch with whom he had a brief affair before becoming engaged to his true love, the young aristocrat Josette du Pres. We see a human Barnabas who is thoroughly decent and likable (he tries to be kind to Angelique while rejecting her), and Angelique becomes the new source of the evil in the series, taking on the traditional soap opera "bad girl" role. When Barnabas becomes a vampire he struggles with his urges, though he cannot conquer them. He is so appalled by what he has become that he asks his devoted servant Ben to stake him, but Ben is prevented by yet another magic spell. By the time we return to 1968, Barnabas is a considerably moderated character. After this return to the present he begins to slowly escape the curse.

Dark Shadows left the erotic qualities of the vampire implicit; as a daytime drama it always dealt with sexuality mediated through romance. Barnabas was at the center of multiple love stories: his love for the lost Josette, his unrequited love for Vicki Winters, his love for Maggie Evans, Julia Hoffman's unrequited love for him. The most dramatic love story of the series involves the witch Angelique's enraged, savage passion for Barnabas compelling her to pursue him across centuries, destroying (or trying to) those who might stand between Barnabas and herself. Angelique became an oddly sympathetic character even though she did horrendous things because audiences understood that she really did love Barnabas, who had, after all, left her for another woman. By the end of the Barnabas storyline, he accepts that he has always loved Angelique, and that she has always really loved him, however many tortures she has inflicted upon him. This happy reconciliation is short-lived, though, as she dies saving his life. All this meant that Barnabas's emotional life, which was completely shaped by his struggle with vampirism, was as exposed as any of the human characters', revealing his vulnerability and his capacity for suffering.

Dark Shadows became the story of a vampire turning into an image of humanity as Barnabas changed over four years from a deadly menace to the savior of the Collins family. Unlike Dracula, Barnabas aspired to what the audience wanted—to be free, to be loved, to be part of a family—and his decades as a vampire were the criminal past he needed to escape to attain these things. As Barnabas is gradually liberated from the horrors of vampirism (even after he is cured there is always the danger that he will revert, either because of the medical treatments' failure, a magic spell, or the effects of time travel) he becomes an emblem of humanity. But just as being a vampire was Barnabas's terrible secret, the secret of *Dark Shadows* was that although the vampire was never glorified, the viewers were interested in Barnabas and identified with him because of—rather than in spite of—his vampirism (however reluctant). In fact, the audience's real secret was that they could never want Barnabas to be cured, for then he would be merely an ordinary man.

Barnabas's evolution was shaped as much by the nature of television as by the appeal of the vampire. The fan reaction to Jonathan Frid's Barnabas was rooted in the kind of experience we expect from a television series. Television stories don't rest their appeal on action or spectacle but on the viewer's relationship with the characters; there had to be some overt identification with Barnabas for the series to work. A stark battle between good and evil, living and undead, provides an excellent dynamic for a movie or novel, which needs a decisive conclusion. But a television series, particularly a daytime drama, relies on keeping the story going; its structure is, in effect, all middle. Thus, Barnabas had to be a character with human emo-

Barnabas, noble protector of the Collins family.

tions and feelings to sustain the endless interpersonal exchanges that are the center of television stories.

Dark Shadows recreated not only the vampire but the traditions of nineteenth-century Gothic and supernatural stories. As *Dark Shadows* careened through time and space, it added to the vampire mix with werewolves, warlocks, a Victor Frankenstein character named Dr. Eric Lang and his monster named Adam, a disembodied head, and a version of H.P. Lovecraft's "Old Ones" called "the Leviathans."[3] Four groups of episodes are set in the nineteenth or late eighteenth century, including one story line in an alternate nineteenth-century universe in which Frid plays Bramwell, the son of a Barnabas who never became a vampire but died peacefully in his sleep.

With this episodic time travel, *Dark Shadows* recovered the past—though doubtless some viewers had no idea how the writers were cannibalizing nineteenth-century literature—in a way that, while retaining a familiar outline, expanded the boundaries of the daytime series to include violence, obsession, the supernatural, as well as emotions such as terror and horror. In one way this made the series completely sealed off from contemporary reality; not only was it full of supernaturalism and monsters, but sometimes it took place in the previous century. But in fact its anachronism and fantasy, the spectacle of Barnabas's struggle with his vampirism and the other characters' clashes with forces of passion and turbulent magic, the sense that it was a radical experiment in the most conservative of mediums, placed it centrally in the spirit of its era.

The series brought supernaturalism and sensationalism together with a brooding sense of a claustrophobic, frightening world while also affirming home, family, and the desire to do good. It would be useless to try turning the over two thousand episodes into a "position." Its underlying values of love and family were completely conventional, but they existed only as unreachable ideals and were never what the series was about. *Dark Shadows* created a mood and attitude about what it meant to be human, asserting that the world and people were more dangerous and irrational, that normality was far more fragile than we wanted to imagine. As Julia says in one espisode, "I no longer know what is right and wrong; I only know what is necessary." *Dark Shadows* made it clear that the frameworks through which we had been imagining the world and our identities were breaking down; the vampire became the image of humanity caught in that sense of framelessness.

An immediate descendent of *Dark Shadows* was *Blacula* (1972),[4] the first of two films about the vampire Mamuwalde. Mamuwalde's story, like Barnabas's, begins in the late eighteenth century then jumps to the 1960s.

Mamuwalde is an African prince who has come to Europe to seek help in ending the slave trade. (William Marshall, the actor who plays Mamuwalde, suggested making the character an antislavery crusader.) Unfortunately he stops at Dracula's castle; the Count reveals himself to be a racist as well as nosferatu and attacks Mamuwalde, who he turns into a vampire. He rapes Princess Luva, Mamuwalde's wife, leaving her to die. Like Barnabas, Mamuwalde remains chained in a coffin until 1965, and then two interior decorators buy Dracula's furniture (I'm not making this up) and take it to New York. There Mamuwalde meets Tina, who is the exact image of his lost Luva. He turns her into a vampire so they can be together, but she is staked, and a devastated Mamuwalde commits suicide by walking into the sunlight.

Mamuwalde, like the later versions of Barnabas, is good natured; as played by Marshall, he is a noble character of considerable dignity whose vampirism afflicts him like a disease, and he detests what he has become. While Mamuwalde owes a great deal to Barnabas, he is also a cousin of Melvin Van Peeble's Sweet Sweetback of *Sweet Sweetback's Baadasssss Song*, the criminal turned revolutionary who became the model for the heroes of blaxploitation movies of the 1970s. While *Dark Shadows* was part of an amorphous moment of liberation and transformation that manifested itself in its revision of the daytime drama form, *Blacula* has an explicitly political subtext. The opening of *Blacula* equates the curse of vampirism with the curse of slavery, the bloodsucking Count Dracula paralleling the European slave trader. Mamuwalde, then, stands for the divided nature of the contemporary black hero, a character forced into crime and violence by his situation in racist America, an image of a larger African American tragedy of lives lost and blighted by slavery. The movie's final scene is clearly tragic, as Mamuwalde, aware of the inescapability of his condition, accepts his death after the second loss of his beloved. In this, the movie is as elegiac as it is liberationist, but at its core is the assumption that the audience, though not the other characters, will see themselves and their situation in the vampire.

Dark Shadows went off the air in 1971, probably because of a combination of declining ratings, relatively high production costs, and creative exhaustion.[5] By that time it was no longer a vampire series, and the loss of that central figure had a decisive effect in the series' loss of vitality. Like the Hammer films, *Dark Shadows* had no particular social or political goal in mind; it was the work of television professionals anxious to expand the boundaries of their medium and genre, though Dan Curtis is particularly devoted to telling horror stories. The task required that they think about how the vampire story could work in this format, which meant making it contemporary in its underlying sensibility. Their collective effort established firmly the possibility that the vampire could be a protagonist, an image of true humanity. The next step in this exploration of the vampire is Anne Rice's *Interview with the Vampire*, which moves from reluctant to enthusiastic vampires.

Gorgeous Fiends

It is through the novels of Anne Rice that the vampire as a vampire became a protagonist. *Dark Shadows* protected the viewer from the full implications of the vampire protagonist because Barnabas so desperately wanted to be cured; being a vampire brought him only pain, however fascinating it made him. The publication of *Interview with the Vampire*[6] changed all this, in part because Rice took the step of asserting that the vampire is a kind of celebrity; after all, interviewing is what we do with celebrities in the hope of discovering the secret of their success, the key to their specialness. Rice's lonely and damned vampires struggle for the freedom that comes with self-acceptance of specialness, difference, and darkness, rather than the return to "normality." This form of liberation has nothing to do with progress or utopia, only with the freedom to be continually engaged in the drama of the self. A blurb from the Boston Globe quoted on the cover of *The Vampire Lestat*, "Her refugees from the sunlight are symbols of the walking alienated, those of us who, by choice or not, dwell on the fringe," summarizes the perspective of the novels exactly. The resonance of these vampires is obvious in the almost cultlike status they have for many people.[7]

Rice turns the cautionary tradition of the vampire story upside down. At the end of *Interview*, the boy who has heard Louis's story rejects its conclusion sees as a cautionary tale of loss and despair. "I don't accept it!" he tells Louis.

> "Don't you see how you made it sound? It was an adventure like I'll never know in my whole life! You talk about passion, you talk about

longing! You talk about things that millions of us won't ever taste or come to understand. And then you tell me it ends like that. I tell you . . ." And he stood over the vampire now, his hands outstretched before him. "If you were to give me that power! The power to see and feel and live forever!"

The vampire's eyes slowly began to widen, his lips parting. "What!" he demanded softly. "*What!*"

"Give it to me!" said the boy, his right hand tightening into a fist, the fist pounding on his chest. "Make me a vampire now!" he said as the vampire stared aghast.

What happened then was swift and confused, but it ended abruptly with the vampire on his feet holding the boy by the shoulders, the boy's moist face contorted with fear, the vampire glaring at him in rage. "This is what you want?" he whispered, his pale lips manifesting only the barest traces of movement. "This . . . after all I've told you . . , is what you ask for?"

Louis's warning has cast the glamour of adventure, passion, and longing upon the boy, involuntarily doing what Ruthven, Carmilla, and Lee and Lugosi's Dracula intend: seducing him and, presumably, the audience. The romance of the vampire, particularly because of the sense of loss, of despair, of failure, becomes the fullest expression of the self, the only real experience of our true identity; to accept these things is to accept everything. To be the outsider is to be truly human, though ironically Louis himself does not see this. The acknowledgment of one's difference from others is the experience of the most real and beautiful self; living with it, whatever the consequences, is being truly free. What vampires have, even Louis, though he appears to hate it, is an intimacy not just with violence or sex but with themselves. Whatever Louis says, this is the central meaning of the novel, and certainly of its successor. Lestat, the vampire who "brings over" Louis in *Interview*, becomes the narrator of the second novel in the series, *The Vampire Lestat*, glorying in his vampirism, proclaiming himself a "gorgeous fiend."[8] The nine years between Louis's and Lestat's voices are marked by a radical change in the status of homosexuality and other forms of forbidden sexuality in the United States. While still marginal and taboo, these lifestyles receive considerably more openness and acceptance. Lestat's aggressive self-glorification, as opposed to Louis's melancholy aestheticism, is part of that changing social climate and attitude.

In Rice's novels, vampirism stands for all that is forbidden but, paradoxically, also natural. The struggle for true self-intimacy and freedom is the struggle to accept the natural even when it is dark, dangerous, and forbidden. In addition to being cautionary tales in reverse, Rice's stories are initiation novels in which the initiate does not return to the "normal" world but remains with whatever strange and menacing secret he has discovered. While vampirism can stand for any secret, in Rice's work it typically represents forms of tabooed sexuality. Becoming a vampire means awakening to and accepting one's own secret nature—whatever is there but has been repressed, especially one's sensual, sexual nature. Rice offers no path to contentment in such self-acceptance, though. When Louis becomes a vampire (or, as it is easy to allegorize, realizes that he's homosexual) he must learn how to live with himself, and he never becomes fully reconciled to his new condition. But this is what makes his self-awareness so exquisite and acute.

From one point of view, Rice's novels, particularly *Interview,* extend the strategy of the Hammer films: they hide the sexuality of the vampire in plain sight. Indeed, part of the genius of *Interview with the Vampire* is its making the sexual subtext so transparent yet completely unacknowledged. But unlike the Hammer films, in which the secret of sexuality the story is openly displayed on the screen, in Rice's work sexuality (whether homosexuality or sadomasochism) is not the "real" subject of the novel. Instead it is another image of inner reality, a secret that, like vampirism, is emblematic of intimate secrecy of all kinds, the vampire narrators' inner life. Their "love of damnation," as Louis calls it at one point, is the emotional center of the novels, the romance with the self, the desire to experience one's own desire, the awareness of oneself as special and corrupt at the same time, fully accepting that state of being.

When I read Rice, I often find her work maddeningly slow and indirect rather than "voluptuous" or "sensuous," as the reviewers call it. Rice's sentences are long, convoluted, and imprecise, her diction a peculiar blend of the "antique" style of the vampires with a modern idiom and syntax. But I think the reviewers and I are responding to the same thing—the way in which Rice's style elaborates the inner monologue of the outsider, the emotional state of feeling different, forbidden, and special, by never actually defining those states. Rice's prose hides in plain sight its real subject, which is the continuous struggle to articulate desires and feelings that can never be made manifest and that, indeed, must remain hidden in order to even exist. The interview device itself makes vampirism into an open secret, placing the forbidden outcast at the center of attention not as a monster but in terms of celebrity. This version of the vampire, which reaches its fruition in *The Vampire Lestat,* in which Lestat desires to be a rock star, admired and seen by everyone, and an invisible creature of the night, to reveal himself without revealing himself, is the essence of what Rice does. Her vampires embody a central tension in contemporary America: the desire for celebrity, notoriety, and recognition centered with the awareness that fame leaves one vulnerable and exposed in the desert of public culture, without an identity of one's own.

Rice recognizes that such a sensibility demands an extravagant, melodramatic, self-consciously poetic representation, for it's completely bound up in a play of imagination. The sadism, blood, arrogance, and passion of the vampires are in some way a game; read with too much skepticism Rice's novels begin to sound like self-parody; taken too seriously the prodigal, self-conscious fantasy disappears. Rice, through Lestat in the introduction to *Queen of the Damned,*[9] seems to acknowledge this situation. Lestat tells the reader (he again takes the role of narrator here) that unlike the two earlier books, they shall leave the "narrow, lyrical confines of the first person singular" and enter the world of "the third person" and "multiple points of view." He then goes on,

> And by the way, when these other characters think or say of me that I am beautiful or irresistible etc., don't think I put those words in their heads. I didn't! it's what was told to me after, or what I drew out of their minds by infallible telepathic power, I wouldn't lie about that or anything else. I can't help being a gorgeous fiend. It's just the card I drew. The bastard monster who made me what I am picked me on account of my good looks. That's the long and short of it. And accidents like that occur all the time.
>
> We live in a world of accidents finally, in which only aesthetic principles have a consistency of which we can be sure. Right and wrong we will struggle with forever, striving to create and maintain

an ethical balance, but the shimmer of summer rain under the street lamps or the great flashing glare of artillery against a night sky—such brutal beauty is beyond dispute.

Now, be assured: though I am leaving you, I will return with full flair at the appropriate moment. The truth is, I hate not being the first person narrator all the way through! To paraphrase David Copperfield, I don't know whether I'm the hero or the victim of this tale. But either way, shouldn't I dominate it? I'm the one really telling it, after all.

Alas, my being the James Bond of vampires isn't the whole issue. Vanity must wait. I want you to know what really took place with us, even if you never believe it. In fiction, if nowhere else, I must have a little meaning, a little coherence, or I will go mad.

So until we meet again, I am thinking of you always, I love you, I wish you were here . . . in my arms.

The combination of humor and self-absorption, irony and ingenuousness, the awkward sentence structure and anarchic diction, the combination of self-conscious playfulness and self-conscious anxiety, particularly about not being the center of attention, are all characteristic of the kind of intimacy Rice established with her readers and the way her characters speak, obliquely, to the readers as herself. Without this sense of self, the stories lose their central interest. After leaving the "lyrical confines of the first person singular," the novels become more and more mystical and ponderous, even theological (Lestat meets God and the Devil and starts worrying about his soul), generating a fantasy world that often seems like an unholy fusion of J.R.R. Tolkien and Georges Bataille. In self-consciously extrapolating the "reality" behind the vampire, Rice in effect breaks her intimacy with the self and with the reader. For Rice, there is no reality outside the self; however far one reaches into the dim past, it is all the drama of the self.

The drama of intimacy with the self, one at the center of Rice's novels, can be understood as the aesthetic counterpart to a commodity culture in which acquiring things is a primary way of defining who we are. The sensation of acquisition ("now I own this") creates a momentary intimacy with the self through the object, which is why buying stuff makes us feel good. But this experience fades. (I think of a cartoon I saw once in which a man, standing by the open trunk of his car, which is full of bags and boxes, looks at the packages in his shopping cart and says, "Damn! the same stuff I bought last weekend.") As a fantasy, Rice's vampire sensibility can never be completely "acquired"; the true secret self is never fully articulated and the moment of total freedom and full self-acceptance is never reached. The vampires' infinite longing is a consumption of feelings rather than objects. Rice's vampires feed on others, but what actually sustains them imaginatively is their feeding on themselves.

From another point of view, Rice appeals to an adolescent and narcissistic sensibility, a longing for self-dramatization masquerading as the love of damnation; Marilyn Manson, the most theatrical of Goth/Satanist rock musicians, is a live-action version of Lestat. Though the labels of adolescent and narcissistic are accurate, contemporary American society hasn't been able to confine this sensibility by assigning it to the young or the pathological. While Rice didn't cause such an attitude to become part of everyday adult culture, she does give it a fictional archetype, and the popularity of her novels indicates the broadscale appeal of this way of imagining oneself.

But Rice ultimately addresses a central concern of our era: how we create an idea of humanity that allows us to live with our own nature, particularly when everything we are is natural. The desire for love, which runs through all of Rice's work and characterizes both Louis and Lestat, is the desire to find freedom not simply in self-acceptance but in a wider humanity that allows us to recognize each other as something more than celebrities. Because of the dilemma arising from being without a frame that defines the human, Rice's novels speak to the fissure between freedom and the values of love, self-awareness as aesthetic style, and identity as what Lestat can only find in fiction, "a little meaning, a little coherence."

"If I am to be human, I must be involved with humanity"

Chelsea Quinn Yarbro's Saint-Germain is the most fully liberated of all vampires. Yarbro came to the vampire novel as a theorist and historian, aware of the folklore and the nineteenth-century stories, and dedicating *The Palace,* the second novel in the series, to Christopher Lee. *Hotel*

Transylvania, the first novel, concludes with notes explaining her thinking about the vampire. She offers her version of the vampire's characteristics as consistent with a careful reading of the lore, and like Stoker, she makes her vampire out of a real historical person (an eighteenth-century alchemist). She writes the notes as if she wants to leave open the possibility that if Saint-Germain was a vampire he would surely have been her kind of vampire. Yarbo brings her pagan, feminist, and humanist sensibilities to her creation of the vampire, infusing Saint-Germain with qualities she takes seriously, ones missing from almost every other vampire in the history of the tradition. At the same time, she is clearly playful in her attitude toward her vampire. The hint that the real Saint-Germain *might* have been a vampire (after all, she writes, his mystery "even today has not been solved") is an invitation to imaginative playfulness, not a sign that Yarbro really believes in vampires.

Yarbro's vampire protagonists are liberated from the veil of superstitions and ignorance that has surrounded human beings throughout history. Saint-Germain, the ancient vampire who is the hero of the novels (along with Olivia Atta Clemens, who first appears in the third Saint-Germain novel, *Blood Games*),[10] embodies the freedom we would attain should we be liberated from the burden of humanity's evils; this freedom is partly sexual and intellectual, but essentially it is ethical. Yarbro's vampires embody not only an ideal of love between men and women rooted in pagan feminism but also an affirmation of the values of tolerance, reason, and the love of art and beauty as an alternative to a humanity typically lost in fanaticism, cruelty, and greed. Yarbro's vampire protagonists are images of ourselves—not as with Barnabas, of who we fear we are, or as with Rice's vampires, of who we must accept we are, but of who we should become.

When *Hotel Transylvania* was published in 1978, it was subtitled "a novel of forbidden love," though subsequent Saint-Germain novels have been subtitled "a novel of historical horror." The latter seems to have always been Yarbro's preference; I have an autographed copy of *Hotel Transylvania* in which she has crossed out "forbidden love" and written in "historical horror." For Yarbro there is nothing about the love between vampires and humans to make it forbidden; this is love as it should be. Moreover, the "horror" of her preferred subtitle has nothing to do with vampires. Set in prerevolutionary France, Renaissance Florence, Neronian

Rome, the courts of Louis the XIII in France and Justinian and Theodora in Byzantium, among others, Yarbro's vampire stories record human history as a tale of violence and terror far more frightening than any vampire. Within that history the exemplary humanity of Saint-Germain and Olivia appears as both an ideal and image of the human inability to achieve its best nature.

In making Saint-Germain a true hero, Yarbro minimizes his supernaturalness; he's virtually immortal, very strong, and has acute senses, but he doesn't turn into a bat or a vapor. His great intelligence, willpower, and ethical sense are what make him superior to all around him. As an alchemist, Saint-Germain is also a kind of super-scientist, ahead of his time in knowing the natural processes governing the world. He drinks blood only from women who desire his bites, and the blood drinking is almost purely erotic; though it is feeding, it has no predatory qualities. Saint-Germain is the perfect lover: considerate, handsome, sophisticated, and a natural feminist, he clearly likes women as equals and is devoted to his lover's sexual pleasure. Yarbro turns the trope of the demon lover upside down. The ideal of romance in the novels is passionate but civilized, and intelligence, wit, and deep, uninhibited sensuality are the natural expressions of sexuality and mutual love.

Thus, Saint-Germain is barely a vampire by conventional standards, Powerful and authoritative but violent only when justifiably provoked, usually by human stupidity or cruelty, Saint-Germain could as easily have been a sorcerer or, as the stories move around in time, Dr. Who with fangs. He is a vampire because Yarbro wants to rewrite the monster as an ideal and because, as a vampire, Saint-Germain is a melancholy (though not tormented) figure. Almost three thousand years old when the series begins, he has been everywhere and seen everything. Though he loves and is loved in returned, it never truly lasts, as humans must die and vampires cannot have sex; he worries that the fact that his own sexual pleasure is derived from drinking blood, rather than from intercourse, will repel his lovers. His melancholy is also rooted in the cruelty and stupidity he has seen among humans, as he, in effect, waits for humanity to catch up to him in knowledge, aesthetic perception, and ethical sense.

Hotel Transylvania, set in eighteenth-century Paris, is a historical romance written from a feminist perspective. The novel has many of the traditional appeals of the historical romance novel: careful attention to period detail, particularly the clothing of the aristocrats; weaving historical fact with the fiction, since there really was a Hotel Transylvania in Paris at this time as well as a vogue for Satanism among some aristocrats. The historical horror here specifically lies in the threats to Madelaine de Montfort presented by the human men who prey upon women. Yarbro goes beyond the reality of male supremacy in the society by making most of the male aristocrats members of a Satanist cult who rape, sodomize, and torture women before sacrificing them to the Devil. The Satanists pursue Madelaine because her father, who had been in the cult but later repented and retired to the country, promised her to them before she was born. The animalistic evil and sexual perversity typically attributed to the vampire is all transferred to the Satanists. When Madelaine is kidnapped by them, Saint-Germain, of course, rescues her, though not before she is stripped and tortured while her father is raped (we are told later) by a particularly awful Satanist. Saint-Germain finally brings Madelaine over by allowing her to drink his blood (she pleads with him several times before he does so), but this means, as revealed later in the series, that they will not be lovers forever, as vampires can only drink the blood of the living.

As interesting as it is, *Hotel Transylvania* is caught up in playing with the conventions of the historical romance novel through a well-tuned use of excess. Yarbro seems to expect the reader to recognize in reading *Hotel Transylvania* that she has not only recreated the vampire but recreated the romance novel, even parodied it in subtle ways. It is in the second book in the series, *The Palace,* that Yarbro defined the essential Saint-Germain story. While Yarbro doesn't abandon the underlying feminist allegory/fantasy, she widens her sense of the dimensions of the struggle for liberation. Renaissance Florence is an environment Yarbro clearly finds more appealing to her sensibility than prerevolutionary France, and Laurenzo de Medici is a genuinely admirable, even tragic, figure. Though the era of the Medicis is seen in the last moments of its decline, the Republic represents an attempt to create a truly humane culture. Once again the horror is located not in Saint-Germain but in Savonarola, who, after Laurenzo's death, destroys all that is good in the city. For Yarbro, the monk's fanatical moralism, demagoguery, and hatred of art are true Evil—much more so than the somewhat ludicrous Satanism of *Hotel Transylvania.* Savonarola's pleasure- and beauty-hating moralism, rooted in a desire for power as well as his own psychological and sexual insecurity, corrupts not only the civic order but art and sexuality as well. Saint-Germain pleads with his friend Botticelli not to consign his paintings to Savonarola's pyres, but Botticelli has been overcome by Savonarola's preaching. Saint-Germain's rescue of one painting is second in importance only to his rescue of Demetrice, the woman who loves him and has been imprisoned by the crazed monk.

To imagine the vampire, who even Rice portrays as a fiend (albeit a gorgeous one), as the embodiment of reason and decency has a transgressive quality in its aggressive rejection of the conventional view of the vampire. Yarbro, in effect, turns the notion of the vampire as a figure of transgression, as in Rice's novels, on its head by creating a Saint-Germain, who embodies civilized values vampires ordinarily reject, such as restraint, self-control, and respect for human life. The way we have imagined the vampire, whether as demonic, Antichrist, or even gorgeous fiend, is really an image of our limitations. For Yarbro, vampire stories cannot be the revelation of our dark side because human history already reveals it in terrible detail. In using Saint-Germain to remind us that, as Walter Benjamin said, the record of civilization is also a record of barbarism, Yarbro's stance is satirical and hinges on the assertion that the vampire is misidentified as perverse and dangerous because ordinary society is so monstrous and irrational.

Yarbro's novels are mildly didactic, appealing to idealism rather than sensationalism. Focused on the ethical rather than Rice's aesthetic and psychological realms, there is little dramatization of Saint-Germain's inner life; Yarbro hides the inner workings of his soul from us, just as Saint-Germain does from his acquaintances.[11] While Saint-Germain is the center of these stories, the points of view of other characters also offer insights, and though Saint-Germain has an acute aesthetic sense (in every century he is something of a fashion plate) and is an accomplished musician, Yarbro, unlike Rice, sees no need to shape the self in aesthetic form. The work of art is of the greatest value, as is artistic talent, but the aesthetic self is simply a monster like Nero. Yarbro turns away from the drama of intimacy with the self; romantic though he may be, Saint-Germain is an actor in human affairs and history, as opposed to Barnabas, whose life centers around the Collins family and Collinwood, or Rice's vampires, whose primary relationships are with their own kind.

Because Saint-Germain is never able to significantly change the course of human history—at best he typically saves a woman from a terrible fate by bringing her over—he is melancholy in his search across the ages for true love, and the history that gives structure to the novels and Saint-Germain's life echoes this gloom. The violence and terror of human history can't be stopped and the ideal is represented solely by a very unusual vampire. Paradoxically, as historical novels, these stories can never reach the future Saint-Germain stands for; indeed, that future becomes itself a fantasy, just like the vampire. Yarbro's novels imagine human history as the endless struggle to put aside violence and cruelty, to go beyond being predators and hence become lovers, artists, and scientists. In the notes to *Hotel Transylvania,* Yarbro writes that the vampire is always "speaking to some hidden part of ourselves." In a typical vampire story, that hidden part of ourselves is our fundamental desires, what Freud would call the "polymorphously perverse Id." Yet for Yarbro the vampire is not the image of our atavistic past calling out for liberation but our future as truly civilized, truly human, beings.

Liberation's Progress

In the wake of Barnabas, Louis, Lestat, and Saint-Germain, the vampire protagonist became a common figure. P.N. Elrod's Jack Fleming is the most recent of the human vampires to have his own series. *The Vampire Files* begins with *Bloodlist* (1990), which invites the reader to "Meet Jack Fleming. Newsman. Lady's Man. Vampire." [12] Elrod dedicated *Bloodlist* to, among others, Jonathan Frid, happily acknowledging the influence of *Dark Shadows* on her own work, though it's hard to imagine a less self-tormented vampire than Jack Fleming. Fleming, a journalist brought over (by his own choice) by a female vampire/lover, becomes a detective, though he also writes short stories for *Spicy Horror Tales* magazine. Fleming bites only women who are willing lovers; for mere feeding he stops off at the stockyard for a nip at an uncomplaining shorthorn. While Fleming is an attractive, romantic lover, the novels primarily focus on the rational vampire as good man through a variation on the hard-boiled detective story. Philip Marlowe's bitter wit has modulated into Fleming's good humored irony about his own condition and the world in general. Although later in the series Fleming finds his desire for blood getting out of control, overall, the values of good sex, good humor, and reasonableness make these novels an oxymoron, the "sunny vampire series."

In the last quarter of the century, the vampire became not only a protagonist but part of a race, species, or society. If vampires were not the monstrous, anti-Christian spawn of the Devil, they still had to come from somewhere. Though modern vampires are still strange beings with special powers, they have less and less connection to the supernatural and certainly none to Christianity. The motif of a society of vampires existing in parallel with, but unknown to, humans becomes more and more common. Such stories are natural extensions of the liberation of the vampire protagonists, whose great torment is ultimately that they are alone, either wrapped in themselves or waiting for a future that never comes. Freedom is a mixed blessing if one is forever alone. While Barnabas finally becomes part of the human Collins family again, Louis, Lestat, and Saint-Germain remain outsiders; and at the heart of the liberationist ideal is not simply the transcendent self, but that self as part of a community that does not compromise freedom through repression. In stories about the search for community, the battle between humans and vampires, which was a psychodrama in the cases of Barnabas and Louis, becomes a battle for control of the vampire society. [13]

George R.R. Martin's *Fevre Dream* (1982) tells the story of two rival bands of vampires, one good, one bad, whose battle against each other is played out during an 1840s steamboat race on the Mississippi.[14] The story is told through the point of view of Abner Marsh, a human caught up in the battle between Joshua York, the leader of the vampires who want to end their predatory ways, and Julian, the corrupt vampire who wants to adhere to the old-time religion of slaughtering humans like cattle. York parallels Rice's Louis, while Julian parallels Lestat; Martin is likely playing with the facts that his story's time period is roughly contemporary with that of Rice's first vampire novel and the two books have similar settings. A cross between *Life on the Mississippi* and *Interview with the Vampire,* Martin's novel subsumes individual desire and identity, the elements central to Rice's vampires, into the need to define and sustain a community that must choose between being predatory or cooperative. *Fevre Dream* brings together the romantic fascination with the vampire as special outsider and the desire for inclusion in a larger world that gives meaning and direction to such individuality. This motif also reappears in the comic vampire movie *Sundown: The Vampire in Retreat* (1990)[15] and the briefly aired television series *Kindred: The Embraced* (1995).[16]

In Michael Romkey's *I, Vampire* (1990),[17] vampire David Parker describes the vampire as "more than a man, less than a god. Possessed with a great sensitivity to beauty, driven by a compulsion to feast on blood sucked from living mortals. An artist dedicated to creating, a parasite ever watchful for the next victim," the tormenting dualities of the Ricean vampire. Parker is more like Saint-Germain than he is like Rice's vampires, though, and *I, Vampire* is most aptly defined as a fusion of romance and adventure. The novel describes Parker's evolution as a vampire: his introduction into the world of the vampires, who are a race ruled by the society of Illuminati; his love for Princess Tatianna, the beautiful Russian vampire and last of the Romanovs; and his confrontation with Prince Albert Victor, the Duke of Clarence, who proves to have been both a vampire and Jack the Ripper. Indeed, many famous historical figures, including the Borgias and Mozart, appear as vampires in this pastiche of human history that uses the secret world of nosferatu in explaining a wide variety of significant events.

While Martin's, Romkey's, and Elrod's novels imagine the vampire as a man/woman of the world, sophisticated, powerful, and free from ordinary rules and restrictions, the vampire protagonist of Jewelle Gomez's *The Gilda Stories* (1991)[18] is a lesbian black woman who becomes a vampire in 1850 Louisiana while running away from slavery. The novel traces Gilda's search for true freedom and community throughout American history and into the future. As with *Blacula,* vampires in *The Gilda Stories* are not simply romantic outcasts but also political outcasts who are searching for a home in which they will be able to live safely and with dignity. Unlike Martin's warring vampires or the embattled clans of *Kindred,* Gomez's vampires do not stand for the abstract choice society must make between good and evil, predation and cooperation, but for those people American society has literally oppressed. Far less melodramatic and adventurous than Romkey's work and less fun than Elrod's Fleming novels, *The Gilda Stories* are melancholy and didactic in their evocation of the desire for true community.

The vampire protagonist allows Gomez to have a single character experience the changes that occur over a period of two hundred years, including the future, though humans accomplish very little in this time. By 2050, the world has become an ecological wasteland and the rich humans hunt vampires to transfuse their blood so they may live forever; in this story that means killing the vampire who gave them eternal life, a violation of the vampire prime directive. The old human order is effectively destroying itself and creating a new form of slavery. Just when her life seems most desperate, Gilda discovers a community of vampires in South America in the ruins of Machu Picchu. Though the world may continue to destroy itself and the hunters continue to pursue vampires, there is nonetheless a community for Gilda in a place built before conquest by the Europeans, which metaphorically suggests the ancient culture's reclamation of the Americas.

Gomez doesn't exalt the vampire in the manner of Romkey and Rice as the ultimate expression of individualism; Gilda and the others are transgressors not out of a Byronic or Sadean daring, but simply because others will not accept who they are. Gomez wants an image of the vampire that is not weak or victimized, but powerful in a unique, enduring way—someone who is a part of and yet in search of a community. Her vampire's immortality is not solely personal and implies rather the endurance of all those who are at the margins of society, searching for a home. While Gomez's Gilda is far from Rice's neo-Victorian gorgeous fiends, both authors are tuned into the pathos of the vampire's story, the sense of loneliness and difference that is its underlying mood.

Nancy Kilpatrick's 1996 *Child of the Night* [19] brings the sensibility and emotional substance of Rice's novels completely into the romance and domestic story tradition of *Dark Shadows*; Kilpatrick's vampires are thoroughly idealized (imagine the Collinses if they had all been vampires and Barnabas longed to join them, rather than the other way around). Unlike Rice's vampires, they live in happy families and rarely kill, taking only enough blood to allay their hunger. *Child of the Night* is a utopian vision of liberation in which getting in touch with the vampire, specifically as a sexual awakening, leads to a greater, fuller, and happier humanity. The central character, Carol Robins, after much resistance and anger, finds her true sexual nature, her real identity as a woman, and true love through this process.

The novel opens with Carol vacationing in France to get away from Philadelphia in the wake of her husband going back to his lover, Philip, who was a close friend of Carol's. Both men are HIV positive, and Carol is afraid that she too is infected. Aimlessly touring Bordeaux, she meets Andre, an attractive though rather pale man who rudely tries to pick her up: "Big breasts, firm ass, I like that," is his come-on line. Later he attacks her; she fights him off but sees him kill an elderly man who has come to her aid and drink his blood. Carol is terrified that Andre will drink her blood, and when he kidnaps her, she offers to become his sex slave for two weeks rather than be bitten. He takes her to a mysterious chateau where he lives with his vampire family. While two other vampires named Chloe and Gerlinde befriend Carol, Andre is alternately tender and brutal, given to sudden bursts of near-psychotic violence, sometimes caressing her, sometimes making her wear a dog collar and chain. Though she is repelled by Andre's cruelty, Carol finds sex with him deeply exciting. When Carol becomes pregnant she agrees to let the vampires raise the child, but after Michael is born, she tries to run away with him. Andre catches her, takes Michael, and, after drugging and hypnotizing Carol, leaves her with no memory of her time with the vampires.

After seven years of therapy and finally testing HIV positive, Carol remembers what happened and after much searching finds Michael living with the vampires in Montreal. Andre is as bizarre and dangerous in his behavior as ever, and while Carol retains her strange combination of fear, repulsion, and desire for him, she realizes that to be with her son, she must become a vampire. The vampire women advise her to be more seductive with Andre, pointing out that he is essentially a physical being and sexuality is the best way to reach him; when she talks with him she is too blunt and challenging. Upon hearing Andre's story, Carol realizes that he has deep ambivalence about himself as a vampire. When his father became a vampire and tried to bring his mother across, she became fearful and his father lost control, killing her; then he committed suicide by chaining himself in the sunlight. The two lovers Andre has previously tried to bring across both pleaded with him to stop; humiliated by their fear and rejection, he lost control and ripped out their throats. As Andre's soulmate, it is now Carol's task to help him accept himself and learn how to love, just as he awakens in her a deeper and more complex sexuality. Finally, having truly given themselves to each other, Carol and Andre accept their mutual love, as she becomes a vampire.

Child of the Night incorporates vampires so completely into an image of ideal humanity that the story of sexual discovery and emotional torment ends by affirming the traditional ideals of motherhood, domesticity, and family, though these values are blended with a mildly occult feminism and a rather dark, somewhat S and M vision of sexuality. What results is a fantasy of perfectly balanced submission and assertion, exclusion and inclusion, monstrousness and normality. Kilpatrick's vampires are thoroughly modern and offer the promise of happiness and escape from the terrors of contemporary life: depression, sexual confusion, and the threat of AIDS. The vampire world becomes a haven of ideal beings living in a perfect balance of sensuality and love, of male and female identity. Such an idealized vision of the vampire takes us, oddly, back to a fantasy of domesticity and normality in which the quotidian reality of middle-class life fuses with the dream of the vampire. As with all vampire protagonist stories, it presents a world without slayers; but here there is no need for them, as the vampire's final aspiration is not to prey freely but simply to be human.

The Limit of Liberation

In the tales of the vampire protagonists, aspirations to freedom and community are central to the ethical vision of the stories. But these vampires all embody another kind of liberation, the expression of identity through style. To be a vampire is to adopt an appearance, a way of dressing, a way of acting that expresses one's distance from the conventional world. With Lestat, the vampire's style becomes the real liberation, while for a vampire like Saint-Germain his distinctive style of dress and manner is simply the sign of his underlying ethical difference from most humans. In the liberationist vampire story, style serves as the indicator of inner values or character, of the fact that even in their self-division or torment, there is a depth. If the vampire embraces style in the sense of manner and fashion as their only identity, they do become free of all human values, but then they must cease to be protagonists.

The nature of the vampire protagonists means that true liberation will always elude them, unless they are ready, as with Kilpatrick, to return to a life in which they cease, in spirit, to be vampires. Vampires began as monsters and can never quite shake this history, and if they do, they begin to lose their significance for us. The vampire protagonist is ultimately a boundary, not a goal. If the vampire becomes an image of freedom and liberation, it does so only by marking the line beyond which such liberation remains unrealized, a limitation any gorgeous fiend must finally acknowledge. It is in this way, oddly enough, that the fantasy tells the truth about itself.

3

THE DRACULA VARIATIONS: PART I

Though Hammer's use of Dracula in recreating the nineteenth century as a spectacle of sex and violence bears only an indirect relation to Stoker's novel, by using Stoker as a source the studio renewed Dracula and *Dracula* for other contemporary storytellers. But Hammer's combination of a fascinating menace and sexual innuendo was too narrow to be endlessly repeated. From the mid-1970s until the early 1990s the Count was the protagonist in his own story, which is what allowed *Dracula* to become our story. These are not liberationist tales, though. While Dracula's violence is modulated into romance (or in the instance of *Blood for Dracula,* grotesque pathos), only Fred Saberhagen's 1974 *The Dracula Tape* falls into the liberationist line of vampire tales. Stories with Dracula as their protagonist are not just romances but stories about the state of the romance story. Moreover, as Dracula is inescapably a historical figure, these stories are about the process of historical change as measured by the difference between Stoker's novel and these new versions of the Count.

In 1974 the creator of *Dark Shadows,* Dan Curtis, produced a television movie of *Dracula* starring Jack Palance. It was among the first versions to portray Dracula partially as a romantic lover rather than simply as a predator. Curtis's Dracula comes to England in search of Mina, who is identical to his long dead lover. A device Curtis had used in *Dark Shadows,* it became a part of subsequent Dracula stories, including *Love at First Bite* and *Bram Stoker's Dracula*. Palance's Dracula is both the brutal feudal lord and the grieving lover of a vigorous adventure story. While Nigel Davenport's Van Helsing is formally the protagonist, Dracula was an object of sympathy as well as fear for the audience. Palance said that Dracula was the only character he ever played who scared him; reportedly, he became so caught up in the role that he actually bit the actress playing Lucy.

From this point on, Dracula became a durable and complex character in contemporary stories. Increasingly, Dracula variations directly engage the themes of Stoker's novel rather than simply borrowing characters and conventions from it; though only one production, the 1978 BBC six-hour mini-series starring Louis Jordan, actually attempts fidelity to it. Through Paul Morrissey's *Blood for Dracula* (1974), Fred Saberhagen's novel *The Dracula Tape* (1975), the 1979 the movies *Love at First Bite* and *Dracula*, and finally Francis Ford Coppola's *Bram Stoker's Dracula* (1992), Stoker's monster becomes a genuine character. After Coppola's version, the Count begins to return to his role as monster, as we shall see in "The Dracula Variations, II."

Where Are the Wirgins?

Blood for Dracula [1] was originally released in the United States in edited form as *Andy Warhol's Dracula,* the companion piece to Paul Morrissey's *Flesh for Frankenstein* (also called *Andy Warhol's Frankenstein*). Morrissey returned to the classic Universal/Hammer pairing of nineteenth-century monsters. The production of *Blood for Dracula,* shot in Italy with an international cast, began immediately after the conclusion of *Flesh For Frankenstein.* Indeed, Udo Kier had no idea he would be asked to play Dracula until the day the earlier film wrapped. The script was written as they shot the movie, with new pages for the actors to learn every day, which may account, along with the fact that English was a second language for most of them, for the tentativeness in some of the performances. Virtually unseen in its original state until recently, the association with Warhol made it clear that this was an unequivocally contemporary *Dracula,* even a campy *Dracula,* though in fact Warhol had little to do with making the movie. While the title *Andy Warhol's Dracula* captured the vampire for avant-garde art, it did so at the very moment when the avant-garde was absorbing and being absorbed by popular culture. While Morrissey had worked closely with Warhol on experimental films and had used some of the techniques devised in The Factory in making *Blood for Dracula,* both monster movies are deeply indebted to conventional commercial entertainment.

Blood for Dracula, while steeped in the popular tradition, reflects Paul Morrissey's sensibility and ethical perspective rather than the struggle to make the traditional story work as entertainment epitomized by *Dark Shadows.* While *Blood for Dracula* has a very modern sense of irony and absurdity that approaches camp, the movie is essentially a melancholy, if often grotesque, satire, a dispassionate look at the inadequacy of the legendary Count and the traditions and values of the past to deal with a modern world, which offers no replacements for the ethos it renders obsolete. Udo Kier's Dracula is a tortured vampire who, though an object of pity and repulsion rather than fascination, embodies the frailty of human identity. Rather than the powerful, virile Dracula of Christopher Lee, Kier's Count has become a weak shadow dying on the screen.

Blood for Dracula is a beautiful movie; dark, meditative, and deliberate, its color ranges deep and rich without being glossy. The poetry of the movie is all in the style, though, for the story of this Dracula is on one level patently ridiculous. Throughout, the humor and visual beauty are carefully balanced with pathos and a sense of moral emptiness. While we are aware of the humor, the characters, with the possible exception of Dracula, have no sense of how ludicrous they are or how absurd and yet dire their situation is. Much of the movie's effects pivots on the contrast between its serene and subdued visual beauty and the violent, absurd, and grotesque behavior of the characters.

Paradoxically, *Blood for Dracula* makes Dracula a contemporary figure by showing how obsolete he has become in the modern world. While Morrissey has no expectation that people will stop telling vampire tales, *Blood for Dracula* is in effect a "last vampire" story in which the death of Dracula marks the collapse of the past, the wretched fate of a monster of the antique fantasy world emblematizes the end of a historical reality. In the opening of the movie we see Dracula/Kier putting on make-up; we are watching both the actor preparing for his role and Dracula trying to look more "normal." This long sequence establishes our intimacy with the Count but also our distance, as we see that in the modern world the vampire is a role even Dracula has to play. Set in the 1920s, the social transformations implied in Stoker's novel have taken place, though the post–World War I world is far more devastated than anything Stoker could have imagined.

The aristocratic Italian family whose daughters Dracula "courts" is as obsolete as he is but substantially less sympathetic, behaving far more decadently and selfishly. Modernity, represented by the "communist" handyman Mario (Joe Delassandro), is brutal, self-involved, and hypocritical. Mario talks about "waiting for the revolution" but does nothing more than wait, and he uses revolutionary slogans as the rationale for his abusive sexual relationships with two of the daughters (he is both their despised "service boy" and a domineering rapist). At the same time, these two sisters, who are also having sex with each other, are arrogant, superficial, and materialistic, already halfway to being vampires.

Kier has said that he conceived of Dracula as a man who wouldn't hurt a fly if he didn't have to in order to survive, and though the Count becomes tiresome in his whining, as intended, we also have a sense of his desperation. Driven by the need to feed, Dracula is reduced to a purely animal state, but he is more like a perverse rabbit than a mysterious bat or a powerful wolf. In *Blood for Dracula,* vampirism seems to be an inherited family disease like hemophilia or chronic anemia rather than, as with Rice's contemporaneous vampires, a terrifying adventure or an essential part of one's true identity. Kier's Dracula is a sickly anachronism whose diet consists of vegetables and the blood of "wirgins." Wirgins are in short supply in Transylvania, and the ones remaining have become wary of the Count and his family. The rest of the Dracula family is dead, with only Dracula and his beloved sister left. In a scene at once sad and comic, the Countess gets into her coffin and accepts her "death" from starvation. Dracula and his servant Anton, with coffin and wheelchair tied to the top of their touring car, set off to Italy because it is presumed that the good Catholic country, will offer a bumper crop of chaste young women. Unsurprisingly, wirgins turn out to be only slightly more common than vampires.

Blood for Dracula has no interest in the erotic vampire, though one of the sisters seems aroused by Dracula's bite. It's clear that Dracula needs blood as food; at one point he stuffs himself with a piece of bread with which Anton has sopped up the blood of a twelve-year-old girl killed in a car crash. Dracula's brief moments of biting and moaning as he feeds, leading to his throwing up when the unwirgin blood makes him sick, are grotesque rather than erotic. In contrast to Dracula's feeding, the movie has "real" sex scenes between the aristocratic sisters and Mario, though they would seem tame on late night cable today. The humans are cold and indifferent to each other; the spectacle is barely arousing, let alone erotic. The romantic fantasy of vampire sex may look grotesque, but reality is equally inadequate.

Rather than become prey to Dracula, the youngest daughter lets Mario quickly deflower her, while the oldest daughter—who though a virgin has been "spoiled" because she was betrothed to a man who broke off the engagement—gives herself to Dracula. Intelligent, proper, and retiring, she recognizes that, unlike her sisters, she has no more place in the modern world than Dracula. In the final sequence, which is both shocking and hilarious, Mario attacks the count and chops off all his limbs until he is reduced to a bloody, wriggling torso. The eldest daughter flings herself on her helpless lover, and Mario stakes them both, then walks back into the castle with the youngest daughter. Even though this over-the-top bloodfest is partly a parody of Hammer movies' violence, the death of Dracula is clearly the supplantation of something by nothing but the violence and empty rhetoric of the communist handyman.

For all its farcicality, *Blood for Dracula* is dominated by a sense of loss and desolation. The attitude toward the vampire is elegiac, as Dracula is a measure of loss, the sign of decay that pervades the whole movie's sense of the modern world. The contradictory and complex tones of the movie, the alternation between comedy and brutality, between sympathy and revulsion for Dracula, move the viewer toward reflection on the meaning of this legend and on the historical changes the characters talk about. The central theme of *Blood for Dracula* is clearly the loss of the past, specifically the nineteenth century's framework of order and values; what in Stoker's novel was a deadly threat to that order has, in Morrissey's movie, become its severely diminished representative. In a sense, Morrissey anticipates and critiques all of the later versions with Langella, Hamilton, and Oldman, in which the Count becomes a romantic figure of nostalgia. Morrissey's insight is that to be faithful to the novel a Dracula story must be about how the novel is steadily lost to us as it recedes into the past.

"I would rejoin the human race"

The popular revision of the Count commences with Fred Saberhagen's *The Dracula Tape,* a liberated vampire story in which Dracula is protagonist and narrator.[2] *The Dracula Tape* is a witty and clever book, with Saberhagen's Dracula emerging as an essentially well-intentioned fellow, an urbane, live-and-let-live kind of vampire, if somewhat self-serving in his account of events. Saberhagen engages directly with Stoker's novel, quoting sections of it and even having Dracula revise the story incident by incident. Dracula's "death" in Stoker's novel was a trick and he is back in 1975 to await his beloved Mina's rising from the grave to join him as a vampire. In *The Dracula Tape,* Dracula is a romantic hero, though unlike Rice's vampires, he is not tormented or even melancholy and would never think of calling himself a "gorgeous fiend." Dracula loses his Victorian monstrosity to become an ironic, world-weary sophisticate who anticipates Saint-Germain more than he recalls Stoker's Count. The *Dracula Tape*'s true literary model may be John Gardner's *Grendel,* which retells the story of *Beowulf* from the point of view of a humane and sympathetic Grendel.

Saberhagen's Count is a very modern man; indeed, it's the appeal of the modern world, "the murmuring of the telegraph across Europe, the infant spluttering of the engines of steam and internal combustion," that called him forth from his castle in 1897. "I could smell the coal smoke and the fever of a world in change" he says. While waiting for Mina to finally arise from the grave, he tells her grandchildren the "true" story of what happened when he came to England; the story is actually spoken into a tape recorder (an eight track), a sign of the Count and novel's up-to-date quality that both recalls Stoker's use of the phonograph and has become similarly quaint. As Dracula tells it, it seems perfectly natural that Mina fell in love him, drinking his blood willingly, and obvious that Van Helsing and his heroic compatriot hunters are silly hysterics who kill Lucy with their transfusions.

Saberhagen's Dracula is at the same time thoroughly modern and old-fashioned. He's a gentleman, an ideal being who is above the nonsense of the foolish and ill-informed humans. With an open attitude toward sexuality, he rejects repressive Victorian moralism in favor of a reasonable and skeptical turn of mind. The cool, ironic, romantic Count is what every man would want to be and every woman would want. While *The Dracula*

Tape embodies an early-1970s skepticism about authority and official accounts of events, this attitude doesn't have any programmatic or political point beyond expressing the eternal irritation the rational being feels in the presence of irrational ones. Saberhagen's affirmation of Dracula and Mina's love is enclosed within the larger value of the book, the wit of his use of Stoker's novel and the inventiveness of his revision of it.

Dracula is an ideal modern man, his skeptical rationalism balanced by his capacity for romantic love and sexual pleasure. While as with Yarbro this view of the vampire is in a sense radical—that which has been Evil now becomes an ideal—the ideal is itself thoroughly traditional. Though perhaps we can see it only in retrospect, Saberhagen's novel, which offers us a Dracula who has as much in common with James Bond and Sherlock Holmes as he does with Stoker's bloodthirsty Transylvanian nobleman, expresses a nostalgia for the "true gentleman," who is ultimately a creature of the past, not the present. While Saberhagen has gone on to write a series of novels about Dracula (who appears under various pseudonyms), his interpretation of the Count has not become central to our versions of Dracula's story, perhaps because the complete revision of Stoker's character makes him such an ideal that he cannot also be Dracula for us.

Morrissey's and Saberhagen's Draculas are quite opposite in tone, as they have contrasting perspectives on the possibilities of modernity: where Saberhagen is witty, Morrissey is absurd; where Saberhagen is reasonable, Morrissey is elegiac; though both insist on Dracula's humanity. At the same time, they each have a distance from Stoker's novel and the traditional vampire that allows them not only to recreate Dracula but to infuse his story with an ironic sense of the significance of that distance. Saberhagen and Morrissey are both moralists; though they don't force conventional didacticism on their audience, they clearly want these stories viewed at least partly in ethical, if wholly secular, terms. In both versions, the central point is how far we have come from our nineteenth-century past; the underlying concern is that we don't know what to do in the present.

Only the Undead Know Romance

Three films, *Love at First Bite* [3] (1979, starring George Hamilton), *Dracula* (1979, starring Frank Langella), and *Bram Stoker's Dracula* (1992, starring

Gary Oldman), comprise the central line of the romance version of *Dracula*; in each, Dracula and Mina's (or her contemporary replacement in *Love at First Bite*, Cindy Sondheim's) relationship becomes the center of the story.[4] While each movie is about aspiring, through the transcendent experience of love, to reconcile the deadly oppositions of sex and violence, good and evil, darkness and light, unlike *The Dracula Tape*, these stories also confront the troubled state of romance in the late twentieth century.

In these movies, the fear and terror figured in Dracula are no longer the threat of the spiritual predator, the morbid seducer, or even the chaos of sexual desire; sexuality is barely an issue. These movies are about the relationships between men and women and the fate of romance in the contemporary world. If cautionary and initiatory vampire stories portray sex as a source of danger and chaos, presenting love and romance, implicitly or explicitly, as the alternative, these movies characterize romance as both an ideal and the center of the chaos underlying our world. While the two 1979 movies are troubled by the apparent failure of romance, *Bram Stoker's Dracula* saves romance by transforming it into a source of spirituality.

Though the troubled state of romance in the late 1970s reflects changing ideas about gender and pointed feminist critiques of romance as mystification of social conditioning under the guise of idealism, the notion of romantic fulfillment was still a powerful image of humanity's realization and remains so today. Though in American culture romance is usually identified as a central value only for women and despite the conventional assumption that only the action hero defines masculinity, the romantic hero is also an important figure in exploring what it means to be a man. For men, what it means to be a romance hero, a man in love, has become more and more significant as women have struggled to situate love and romance in a new way of understanding themselves. While in their idealization of romance these movies are all nostalgic, they are also characterized by a pervasive uneasiness about its future. The transformation of Dracula into a lover is the work of men; if the Count was the great threat to the men in Stoker's novel or the Hammer films, in these works he has become the great question mark—is this who we are? Who we should be? Who we can be? The attempt to imagine a new relation between masculinity and love appears farcial in *Love at First Bite*, while in the Langella version it is manifested in the strangely ambiguous attitude toward Dracula, an anxious fascination.

"Worth more than all of you combined!"

Dracula (1979), written by W.D. Richter and directed by John Badham, grew out of Frank Langella's Broadway success in a revival of the 1927 Balderston and Deane play but developed into something quite different, diverging even from the adaptation with Lugosi. This is a fundamentally undecidable *Dracula* that makes the Count an inescapably ambiguous figure. Except for the love scene between Dracula and Lucy, the movie takes place in a silvery gray-green dreamland that is also the landscape of a dying Victorian world, implicitly the image of our own decaying fin de siècle time. The movie begins with Dracula's arrival in England and the wreck of the *Demeter* at Whitby. Mina and Lucy have exchanged names: Mina is Van Helsing's daughter, Lucy is Seward's, and ready not only to marry Jonathan Harker but to become a lawyer herself in the firm of Snodgrass, Schilling, and Wallop. Jonathan Harker is still Dracula's solicitor but has never been to Transylvania, having conducted all business by letter. Richter's reshaping of the story makes for a cleaner narrative line that places Lucy clearly at the center of the story. A self-confident, assertive modern woman, Lucy is attracted to the Count because he is the most exciting man in her world. She is enchanted, perhaps literally, because he offers her what Snodgrass, Schilling, and Wallop (and Jonathan Harker) don't: a transcendent romantic magic.

At the very beginning of the movie Dracula has preyed upon Mina, who is a sweet but sickly young woman rather than the self-centered sexual fantasist of Stoker's novel, feeding on her immediately after the *Demeter* is wrecked. He has hypnotically wiped all trace of this from her memory though not from her body; within a few hours, Mina has begun to look distinctly corpselike. Upon turning into a vampire, she is hunted by her father and Dr. Seward in an abandoned mine, she appears grotesque and perverse, her body a rotting, deathly white as she tries to seduce/bite her father. Mina has become an unnatural abomination, but Dracula never appears in such a form, though he does morph into a bat and a rather handsome wolf.

Later Lucy goes to Dracula and apparently willingly becomes his lover; she also seems more than willing to be transformed into a vampire. The scene in which he bites her and she drinks his blood is surreal and symbolic; rendered in a fiery red and yellow, the stylized realism of the rest of the movie is abandoned in favor of a montage that shows Lucy and Dracula beyond human space, time, and consciousness in a realm sharply contrasting with the half-lit human world of the rest of the film. When Van Helsing, Harker, and Lucy's father prevent her from going to Dracula she proclaims him "kind and sad" and of more value than any of them. Dracula tells Van Helsing that he loves Lucy and will make her the first of all his brides, promising she will have power over the souls and bodies of the living, so it seems he has some sort of feeling for her. He even offers to spare the rest of the humans in exchange for her being allowed to go with him. Any thoughts of making England into the Empire of the Undead are abandoned in favor of romance.

But we are never sure that Lucy's love for Dracula is not an illusion, because we see another, quite different perspective of Lucy's attitude toward Dracula. Sedated and locked in her father's asylum after she is prevented from rejoining Dracula, Lucy attempts to bite Harker. When Van Helsing backs her off by thrusting a cross at her, the signs of vampirism disappear and she weeps, reaching out to place the cross on her cheek. When the host touches Mina in Stoker's novel it burns her, but here Lucy is able to embrace the spiritual image that has terrified her seconds earlier. This scene seems to suggest that Lucy, like Mina, has been hypnotized and loves Dracula only under a spell.

The ending of the movie is equally ambiguous. Dracula "rescues" Lucy and they escape from the asylum to return to Transylvania. Harker and Van Helsing catch up with them just as the ship is putting out to sea. In the ensuing fight, Van Helsing is stabbed, perhaps mortally wounded, with his own stake when Lucy calls out to him not to kill Dracula. Harker, reduced to using a gun, looks like he will fail, allowing Dracula to escape with a willing Lucy. Van Helsing manages to catch the Count with the hook of a winch and hoist him out of the ship's hold and up to the mast where, hanging in the sunlight, he begins to burn to death. Lucy looks up to see him twisting against the sky, and once again the signs of vampirism fade. Then, as the cape detaches from the mast, it seems to fly away like a

Dracula (Frank Langella) puts the whammy on a garlic-wielding Van Helsing (Laurence Olivier) in Universal's 1979 *Dracula.*

bat. Somehow Dracula has survived the sunlight and escaped, and a smile evocative of her vampirism comes over Lucy's face.

Such an ending typically serves as the set-up for a sequel in the old Universal/Hammer tradition. In this movie, though, it is part of the purposeful ambiguity of the film. The horror of Dracula is quite real, as is Lucy's desire to be restored to humanity. But Dracula is also a figure of great romantic power and force, and Lucy's desire for him is real, too. Dracula robs Lucy of her own will and yet fulfills her desires; accordingly, she is both the most independent and contemporary figure in the movie as well as the most traditional one, swept off her feet by the mysterious stranger, the demon lover.

By supporting at least two quite different senses of romance, Richter and Badham make Dracula and his story, and Lucy and hers, undecidable in their meaning. Notwithstanding his magical appeal, we never know for certain who Dracula really is or whether Lucy really loves him or is simply under his spell. The spiritual values the movie invokes in the form of crosses and hosts are tokens, and only Van Helsing, who worries about his daughter's soul, seems concerned with such things. The spiritual values the story supports are literally pale before the burning heat of passion; the real world is a wan, gray place; nothing else in the world offers the vibrancy of the vampire romance. The transcendent romanticism of Dracula and Lucy's passion transfigures them but does nothing to alter the essentially predatory cruelty and brutality of vampirism. If the visual quality of the movie evokes a dying Victorian world, then the romantic possibilities offered by Dracula, even with his brutality, become a plausible choice. But this romantic possibility is beyond any ethic or any place in reality. The romantic love that Lucy and Dracula embody is beyond our understanding, isolating the lovers in an unknowable realm. By making the vampire into a romantic figure, romance itself is rendered in uncertain terms, for though the vampire is no longer simply a figure of evil, he remains a figure of danger.

By refusing to offer clear answers to any of its questions, this *Dracula* turns the story back upon the audience. One must make of this movie what one wants, and so Dracula becomes our mirror. The possibility of spiritual values is held out, but the value of an ominous romanticism is what the movie lingers upon. In this *Dracula* the romance story has lost its coherence, for we cannot know if romance is a dangerous illusion or a transcendent alternative.

"I Love the Night Life"

George Hamilton's *Love at First Bite* wants us to know for certain that this is a contemporary Dracula, so we see the Count in a disco dancing to Alicia Bridges' "I Love the Night Life." *Love at First Bite* is a comic farce, as opposed to Morrissey's grotesque one, contrasting a romantic yet absurd Dracula with urban New York in the late seventies. Hamilton, hammily parodying Bela Lugosi's Dracula, transforms the vampire's monstrousness into comic strangeness, making him very sympathetic. Feeling out of place and obsolete, he's a forlorn creature, a once-terrifying legend caught in a world in which a fearsome bat is seen as a black chicken and drinking blood from a wino gives even the King of the Undead a hangover. While as with Stoker's Count the human world defeats him, it does so not through courage or goodness but simply by its pathetic vulgarity. Yet, unlike Stoker's Count, he survives his defeat because he believes in romance.

Hamilton coproduced the movie, and the script undoubtedly reflects his own ideas about romanticism (and his own romantic allure, though it must be said that Dracula is his best role). Makeup and accent aside, this Dracula is a seductive lover who takes Cindy Sondheim, the reincarnation of his lost love (played by Susan St. James), away from a meaningless life of one-night stands, drugs, and an empty relationship with her neurotic psychiatrist boyfriend Jeffrey Rosenberg (born Jeffrey Van Helsing, grandson of Dr. "Fritz" Van Helsing). As a model and disco-enthusiast, Cindy lives most of her life at night anyhow, so flying away into the night with Dracula, however ludicrous, is clearly her liberation from the horror of modernity.

Despite the extraordinary difference in mood and tone, *Love at First Bite* deals with the same issues as the Langella *Dracula*. Hamilton's imitation of Lugosi is equally ambiguous, as it is not only comic and romantic but has an underlying note of pathos. What saves Dracula in this movie, unlike in *Blood for Dracula,* is his determined refusal to accept that he is obsolete combined with our awareness that Hamilton is mocking his own screen persona. If Langella's Dracula is a masculine conundrum, Hamilton's masculinity is a series of ironic self-burlesques. The New York of *Love at First Bite* is ugly and silly, an empty world without even the wan beauty of *Dracula*'s dying nineteenth century; romance is the only real alternative.

Romance in *Love at First Bite* is something out of a legendary past, and while antique and silly, it's clearly better than anything in contemporary America. The combination of farce and nostalgia, while often amusing in its goofy way, has an oddly similar effect as the open-ended ambiguity of the Langella *Dracula*. While in that film the undecidability of what Dracula represents takes on a serious and ominous tone, in *Love at First Bite* the use of farce to express nostalgia illustrates the conceptual incoherence of the vampire romantic comedy, however well the movie hangs together as we're watching it. The producers know that these romantic ideals are part of a world that only existed in literature and movies. The romantic ideal is a farce, the vampire is a farce, but the modern world is also a farce. The question is which farce we prefer. As is always the case with such self-conscious meta-stories, it turns out that we prefer the world we imagine to the world we live in, even when we know it's ridiculous.

George Hamilton as the Count in *Love at First Bite* (1979).

While *Love at First Bite* doesn't seem as if it would support a serious sense of romance as a problematic ideal, especially since Cindy and Dracula fly off together as bats, happy creatures of the night. But this farcical ending is only happy in a formal way. We certainly feel the pleasure of this comic resolution, but it doesn't have any real force behind it in way that the happy endings of comedies usually do. If you can only have romance with the undead, then romance is dead. The ambiguous or farcical Draculas of these movies become images of our own state, awful or indecipherable fantasy images of the identities we can no longer imagine for ourselves. Our sense of Evil—the vampire—and our notion of the Good—romance—have lost their clarity, and we cannot be sure what our stories tell us, for they end in either ambiguity or absurdity.

Godfather of the Undead

While earlier Dracula stories examine the unraveling of a culture and its legends—a process to which the stories contribute—in *Bram Stoker's Dracula*, Coppola wants to knit this fabric back up. Throughout his work, Coppola has been concerned with the loss of the past and the sense of order and value embodied in tradition. In the *Godfather Trilogy, Apocalypse Now, Gardens of Stone,* and *Tucker: The Man and His Dream,* the corrosive effects of modern society endanger the things he values most: family, love, and art. Coppola's *Dracula* is not an elegy for what has been lost in the hundred years since Stoker wrote his novel, though. While Coppola and screenwriter James Hart revise Stoker's novel in significant ways, *Bram Stoker's Dracula* tries to achieve the fidelity implied in the title by recovering the central spiritual values of the novel in contemporary form. The advertising slogan "Love Never Dies" and the Annie Lennox song on the soundtrack, "Love Song for a Vampire," make it seem that this is another movie about romance. And although the story of Dracula and Mina is a romance, the power of love in this movie goes beyond a happy or ambiguous romantic ending. In *Bram Stoker's Dracula* true humanity is found not in sexual freedom, self-acceptance, or transcendent love, but in the acceptance of loss, sorrow, and limitation. Romance becomes the route to spirituality and affirms the possibilities of human transcendence through a love that is morally ennobling because it is deeply painful. Even more than romance, though, Coppola affirms the positive ethical and aesthetic qualities of nostalgia as a mode of creating value.

Bram Stoker's Dracula is an opulent, operatic, excessive movie; the visual style is eccentric by mass-release standards, frankly surreal, and just complex enough to be unusual without seeming avant-garde. Coppola erases the conventional lines of time and space, the division between physical and mental realities; he superimposes images, dissolving from one iconic form to another; he uses a self-reflective editing style and builds a meta-narrative by revisiting such silent era techniques as the iris dissolve, which convey meaning visually rather than through dialogue or action. For instance, while Anthony Hopkins's Van Helsing is vivid, he is never developed or really introduced; he simply appears in a scene in the dissecting theater and then bustles about staking and beheading during the rest of the movie. Indeed, *Bram Stoker's Dracula* could easily have been a silent movie.

Bram Stoker's Dracula tells the story of a man lost to power and violence who is saved by love. To be truly faithful to Bram Stoker's novel, Coppola makes two substantial changes. In Gary Oldman's performance, Dracula becomes not merely sympathetic but tragic. Coppola expands and transforms the lost love plot of *Dark Shadows,* Curtis's 1971 *Dracula,* and

Gary Oldman as the aesthete's Dracula in *Bram Stoker's Dracula* (1992).

Love at First Bite, presenting Prince Dracula as feudal warrior, monster, aging decadent, modern dandy, and suffering beast. Oldman's Count suffers because of the loss of love: not simply the loss of his beloved wife Elizabeta but the loss of God's love. Dracula's vampirism stems not from a pact with the Devil for victory over the Turks (as in Stoker's version) but from his rage when the church denies that his wife, who has committed suicide thinking he died at battle, can be at peace in heaven. Insane with grief that he shall never be with her again, he attacks the cross; cursed, he is drenched by endless gouts of blood. Dracula's violence and rage are rooted in his exclusion from both romantic and spiritual love, which for Coppola are two sides of the same sentiment. The pious, if brutal, defender of the faith becomes a monster but finds the possibility of redemption in Mina Harker, who looks exactly like the dead Princess Elizabeta.

Coppola accepts the modern transformation of the relations between men and women by making Mina the central ethical actor, the person who truly understands the spiritual nature of Dracula's situation, rather than a maternal inspiration to the men around her. She neither is hypnotized by Dracula nor, as in the novel, feels merely a Christian pity for him; Mina truly loves him, desires him sexually, and is ready to be unfaithful to Jonathan with him. While Stoker embodies the spiritual power of love within a non-sexual, familial band of heroes organized around the icon of Mina, Coppola has Mina alone perform the decisive act of the movie. Weeping, she kills Dracula because she loves him—she has indeed offered herself to him—and must set his spirit free, turning the power of violence into an act of liberating love and redemption.

As with a Hammer film or the 1979 *Dracula,* the world of the 1890s is visually distant from ours: the clothes, decor, and exteriors look strange, even dreamlike. But when Dracula arrives in London and begins his pursuit of Mina after he literally bumps into her on the street, he takes her to the cinematograph; their first date at the movies mirrors the audience's own presence in a theater. Coppola duplicates the look of old movies in the beginning of the scene; he knows that Dracula came into being at the same time as the motion pictures and that for a hundred years they have been his element. Through the scenes in the cinematograph, Coppola shows us our continuity with as well as our distance from the Victorians; they were the end of an era but the beginning of our own. The cinematograph is one of the many ways Coppola visually reminds us that theirs is an era like ours, caught up in technological change. When we read the novel today, the typewriter, the dictaphone, the phonograph have lost their futuristic appeal and, indeed, seem quaintly antique. Coppola revives our sense of the complex and transitional qualities of the era when he shows Mina typing, surrounded by Victorian furnishings and decor.

Bram Stoker's Dracula also gives us the Victorian world we've come to believe in, the one beneath all the clothes and formality that was deeply obsessed with sex. Drenched in rich reds and golds, hazy and glowing, or dark and electric, the screen pulses with an erotica of color and visual detail, the kind of erotica with which Coppola is most comfortable. The Lucy of this film is without inhibitions and totally absorbed by her sexuality. When Quincey Morris arrives at a party she bounces up to him squealing about how she wants to see his "big knife," which she snatches from its sheath, apparently yanking it right out of his trousers. Even the "pure" Mina looks at an illustrated edition of Burton's *Arabian Nights,* full of drawings of oddly flexible turbaned gentlemen and veiled ladies having sex in a wide variety of positions. While Lucy proclaims her delight, admitting these are her fantasies, Mina *says* she is repulsed, but we can see this is not completely so.

Thus, while Coppola and Hart appear to agree with the Hammer productions that *Dracula* is largely about sex, sexuality is only the surface concern of *Bram Stoker's Dracula.* As Coppola and Hart know, for today's moviegoer the repression of sexuality no longer exists; there is nothing to be said through innuendo and metaphor. Sex can be represented so directly now that many scenes in *Bram Stoker's Dracula* would have been labeled pornographic thirty years ago. Sexuality isn't the subject of the film's imagery, but it provides images and metaphors that stand for the struggle between power and love, the material and the spiritual. For Stoker, sex was the balance point between human and animal, good and evil, so he made clean and sharp divisions between sanctified sexuality and demonic lust—but Coppola and Hart don't. One fades into the other because for them sexuality itself is not a moral issue. The movie and the novel diverge on this matter.

The sexuality of the vampire is bestial; Dracula appears as a monster, apish and covered with hair or as a deformed, leathery bat-creature. When he kills Lucy he attacks her as a wolf, and her vaguely orgasmic cries are full of pain as the act is an animalistic rape. Yet the images of bestial sexuality do not show its essence but demonstrate what sex becomes when linked with power, rage, and violence. Thus eroticism takes on a completely different significance in the movie than in the novel. Lucy's frank sexuality is downplayed as eagerly adolescent rather than sinful; Dracula brings evil to her and makes sex its vehicle. The suffering Dracula and Mina, who loves him more than she loves her husband, are characters for an era in which sexuality is far from Original Sin.

Coppola affirms that spiritual love can flow directly from sexuality and desire, saving it from deformation by rage and the lust for power. The last shot of the film depicts an ancient painting of Dracula and Elizabeta, two glowing lovers reunited in a heaven that accepts them both. Dracula transcends the merely physical to achieve holy love, literally becoming an icon where once he had become a monster. With Mina killing Dracula out of a love that is both spiritual and sexual, the movie offers a contemporary version of Stoker's Victorian faith in love's spiritual redemption, one that accepts love's intimacy with violence and affirms its ability to transform it.

For both Stoker and Coppola, the power of love lies in sacrifice, in surrendering ourselves for others. Jonathan Harker, recognizing that Mina loves Dracula and must redeem him, lets her go into the chapel with the

Tough Love: Mina Harker (Winona Ryder) stakes Dracula (Gary Oldman) in *Bram Stoker's Dracula* (1992).

monster who tried to kill him. Mina realizes that she must kill Dracula to give him the peace he longs for, so she plunges Quincy Morris's big knife deep into his heart, tugs it out, and slices off his head (tough love, indeed). Prince Dracula finally rejects the physical world he has sought to dominate, seeking the peace that only death and transcendence of the physical can give, surrendering his body to death. Love, for Coppola, means accepting death, accepting the sacrifice necessary to give love meaning.

Bram Stoker's Dracula affirms that we need to be more Victorian—not less—to accept the "true" story of Dracula as our own, rejecting attempts to emancipate us from the past, for such freedom leaves us unable to discern what is truly valuable. In *Bram Stoker's Dracula,* only by returning to the past and its underlying sense of spiritual value can we secure such value in the present. The Victorian tale of *Dracula* envisioned through late-twentieth-century eyes links our modern situation to traditional values. The late-nineteenth-century world of the movie is both then and now, and the saving power of love is, for Coppola, eternal. At the turn of our century we should revisit Stoker's message: spiritual love is what the modern world needs. As is often the case with Coppola, what we need is what we have lost, which now can be retrieved only through art. *Bram Stoker's Dracula* wants to embody such clarity and a sense of hope. At the same time, that value is truly mythic, coming to us in a story of our Victorian forbears, in icons and a glowing religious light that is absent from our world.

4

POST-HUMAN VAMPIRES: "WE ARE ANIMALS"

T he vampires of *Martin* (1976), *Nosferatu* (1979), *The Hunger* (the 1981 novel and 1983 film), *The Vampire Tapestry* (1981), *Vampire's Kiss* (1983), *Habit* (1996), and *The Addiction* (1996) are images of the "post-humanity" we are becoming.[1] The "post-human" vampire is the disturbed and disturbing evil twin of the liberated vampire; while at the center of their stories, they are not protagonists but fill the place left by the absent slayer, who is either missing, ineffective, or uncomprehending. These vampires are not romantic outsiders or gorgeous fiends (though they sometimes look as if they are) but self-alienated, fragmentary beings who cannot define their own identities, feral intellects without a capacity for empathy or an ethic beyond need. While liberated vampires accept the dark side as natural, post-human vampires make a fetish of their own needs, which then rule them.

The post-human vampire has its real-life analogues in the pathological behaviors that have provided such important explanations of human nature in recent years. Sexual obsession (*Martin, Vampire's Kiss*), drug addiction, and alcoholism (*The Hunger, Habit, The Addiction*) underlie the post-human vampires, who are given over to compulsion, creatures without meaningful choice. Having lost control of their bodies they lose their souls—in an era in which we don't even know for sure what that word means. In this sense, the post-human vampire is the dark side of liberation in which desire becomes need, which enslaves instead of freeing. At the same time, the post-human vampire often retains the gloss of celebrity, a visual stylishness that places them, through the metaphor of fashion, at the edge of the future.

"Post-human" refers to the condition arising when we lose a definition of humanity that commands a broad social consensus. This situation, rooted in our loss of faith in both tradition and progress, leaves us to float in an endless now, unrelated to the past but without clarity about the shape of the future. This lack of essence strikes particularly hard in American culture, with its traditions of optimism, faith in progress, and belief in the individual. At the end of the twentieth century the ideal of the individual seems overwhelmed by an increasingly complex society, even though the affirmation of such ideals continues and indeed increases, as seen in the revival of the heroic narrative by popular movies starring Tom Hanks: *Philadelphia, Forest Gump, Apollo 13,* and *Saving Private Ryan.* Such primary ideological uncertainties reflect and underlie the changes in our understanding of gender, race, ethnicity, and sexuality, which remains unresolved. At the emotional core of this situation is a feeling of fear about who and what we really are, which finds expression in the terrors of the vampirism.

Typically, the conception of post-humanity revolves around the assumption that "the human" is an Enlightenment idea that will become obsolete; though it may involve the prospect that we will literally remake ourselves, going beyond nature or begetting our successor species in our wombs of the future, the laboratory and the factory. Science fiction has been the genre that addressed this theme, using the form of robots; androids; cyborgs; AI, the non-biological species surpassing humans as the apex of creation; and sometimes invoking the figure of the superior alien. Today we are quite possibly on the brink of both engineering artificial intelligence and transforming humanity at the level of our biological essence, DNA, which is effectively the scientific version of the human soul. The new beings that may result from this technology terrify us because they will have intellect and power but no link to the past, no natural relation to the world that teaches them right from wrong, not to mention good from evil.

While vampires are not monstrous in the sci-fi sense, they are literally post-human: they were once human and now they are something else. Rather than being a sign of the suppression or transcendence of nature, as an android would be, post-human vampires are the natural unleashed. Pure predators, pure need, vampires may be death incarnate but they also embody the most basic human drive: to live. Vampires reject their place in the cycle of nature, but in this they represent nature exceeding itself; though undead, they are the triumph of the individual survival instinct over death.

The idea of the post-human is a sign of contemporary ontolgical uncertainty: we no longer know what we can call natural or how we can define human nature. Unable to define "nature," we cannot make ethical choices. By imagining the post-human, we seek to define the truly human, experimenting with various concepts of "the natural" in this search. The post-human vampire most often equates nature with primary biological desires such as sex, aggression, and hunger, along with the notion that our intellects are our most distinctive human quality. Post-human vampires are material beings without the need for ethical choice, because their needs and desires define their behavior. In post-human vampire stories, the ideal of identity as pure style returns as pure surface; such vampires have no inner torment, nor do they have souls, not because they have lost them but because they live in a world in which there may be no souls.

While science fiction imagines the terrors of the post-human in the collapse of the natural, vampire stories imagine it in the triumph of human nature, which reflects our recognition that what we naturally are cannot provide us with humanity, a meaningful sense of our identity. Post-human vampires are thoroughly naturalized beings, without the connection to the supernatural we see in *Dracula* or the kind of alternative spirituality manifested in the sensitivity and artistic sensibility of Louis and Saint-Germain. Nature affirmed in this perverse way renders it unnatural; only the social order, not nature, can teach us about humanity. The conservation of humanity will not come from a return to the natural but only from the restoration and recreation of a social order, an ethos rooted in something other than the vampire and nature's eternal "I want."

Triumph of the Predator

Werner Herzog's 1979 *Nosferatu* is a remake of F.W. Murnau's 1922 film, itself a version of *Dracula*. Herzog wants to be in direct dialogue with Murnau's movie; he carefully reproduces shots, even whole scenes, from

83

the original, just as Saberhagen weaves Stoker's text into his own. Though it was released in the same year as the Langella *Dracula* and *Love at First Bite,* Herzog's project with *Nosferatu* is quite different than either of the two American movies. Langella's and Hamilton's Draculas were part of an American dialogue about the collapse of romance and the transformation of intergender relations that sought to retain romance as a value even while recognizing that it was in a literally morbid decline. Herzog's more extreme perspective is frankly apocalyptic.

In *Nosferatu,* the real, complete, and profound failure of love between Lucy and Harker mirrors a society conquered by death and chaos; the vampire becomes the image of the new man who arises, strong and forceful, on the ruins of that world. In the 1922 film, Ellen (the Lucy/Mina character) sacrifices herself to save the community from the vampire by allowing him to feed on her until he is caught in the sunlight and fades away. Herzog revises Murnau's scene by having Ellen's sacrifice fail. Though Dracula is wounded by the sunlight and killed when Van Helsing drives a stake into his heart, the plague does not end. When the surviving members of the town's hierarchy come to arrest Van Helsing for murder, it becomes clear that the entire structure of the community has been destroyed, perhaps irreparably. Worst of all, Jonathan Harker becomes a vampire, riding off to continue the reign of terror begun by the Master. Indeed, since Dracula had come to hate his blighted and pointless existence, Jonathan, an energized vampire full of purpose, is more dangerous than the Master.

In Murnau's movie, Orlock is a rail-thin, rotting monster with rat fangs, bat ears, sunken eyes, a hairless dome of a head, and immense hands tipped by long, pointed nails. There is nothing even vaguely sympathetic in this character; he is visually associated with the rats who bring a plague to the town along with him, and he is little more than disease in human form. By 1979, Orlock has changed. Klaus Kinski's Dracula is even more pathetic and grotesque than Kier's, seeing his "life" as meaningless, longing to die, and yearning for the love he has lost along with his humanity. In a small but significant departure from Murnau, Kinski's Count not only bites Lucy's neck but rests his hand on her breast while he does so. It's barely sexual, let alone erotic, but shows how this pathetic act is all that is left of sex and love for the vampire.

If Badham and later Coppola, reflecting their own romanticism, chose to make their movies visually beautiful, Herzog's color seems muted and his images subdued. The romanticism remains but in a minor key, melancholy and skeptical. The camera's position is typically cool and distant, and Herzog makes no effect to give the images the glossy eroticism used by Badham and Coppola. Quite exquisite in its own way, *Nosferatu* has a plain style that juxtaposes careful composition and realistic detail with surreal moments, such as the bizarre geometry of the lines of coffins carried through the town square, which later becomes a grotesque outdoor asylum full of all the people driven mad by the horror of the plague.

At the center of this movie is a sense of complete moral failure and social disorder. What appears in the beginning to be a serene nineteenth-century world turns into a disaster zone. The opening credits are superimposed over shots of mummified corpses looking as inhuman as Dracula. At first, for an American viewer, the opening signals that the movie is about death and decay; but as a German movie, *Nosferatu* gives these bodies an historical meaning: they look like those in films of the concentration camps. The movie is partly an historical allegory about the infection of romantic idealism passed on to the fascists of the twentieth century; Bruno Ganz's loving Harker transforms into the purposeful Nazi, the death's head who races off about his horrific business. Herzog emphasizes this by using the music from Wagner's *Das Rheingold,* recalling the Nazi affinity for Wagner and linking the vampire to Albrecht, the dwarf who renounces love to obtain the ring.

This allegory would have been particularly forceful for German audiences, as Ganz himself was identified throughout the 1970s as the archetype of a new, sensitive German man, the antithesis of the Nazi or the Prussian. *Nosferatu* is part of the recreation of the past undertaken by filmmakers like Herzog and Fassbinder in the 1970s to remind Germans of the realities of the Third Reich. As in *Fitzcarraldo* and *Aguierre, The Wrath of God,* Herzog tells the story of modern Germany through allegory and analogue, emphasizing that the world of the Nazis is not simply part of the past but a state of mind, an attitude that is always there, waiting to return. The use of Ganz especially says that this is not simply a tale of the past but a possibility for the future; a new sensitivity is not an infallible protection. Just as the vampire is implicitly linked to the Nazis, the Nazi terror itself becomes an implied metaphor for the horror of the future.

Dracula (Klaus Kinski) and Mina (Isabella Adjani) share a tender moment in Werner Herzog's 1979 remake of *Nosferatu.*

Kinski's Dracula is beyond any romanticism, and no one could liken him to the handsome, suave figures cut by his 1979 Dracula contemporaries, Hamilton and Langella. He signifies the loss of something larger than the individual romantic possibility, though his grotesque state very much reflects the consequences of such a loss. Dracula's inhuman appearance represents the loss of the possibility of sustaining value of any kind, even in nostalgia. Love is either tainted or ineffectual, and the vampire is the final image of what lies ahead as Harker rides from his village to spread the plague. Herzog's images are apocalyptic because they are linked to the horrors of World War II and the Holocaust, but they are more than lessons about the past. By inviting us to exercise an historical perspective in watching this movie, recalling the history of the vampire story, the history of German cinema, and the history of the twentieth century, Herzog conveys an implicit warning about the future.

"I am not the monster who falls in love and is destroyed. I am the monster who stays true."

In one sense, Suzy McKee Charnas's extraordinary novel *The Vampire Tapestry* makes a radical break with the tradition of the vampire story (the Washington Post review called it "revolutionary"), though it is more accurately a remorseless transformation of the vampire from a supernatural being into a natural one. Charnas's book is dedicated to Loren Eisely, "whose writing first opened to me the vast perspectives of geologic time. From those distances eventually emerged the figure of the vampire as envisioned in this book." The vampire, Edward Weyland, which is only the name he uses for the moment, having no "real" name, is a mutation rather than a supernatural creature, a solitary who knows no others of his kind. Moving through time by long periods of hibernation, he wakes with a knowledge of languages and general survival skills but no substantial recollections of the lives he led before his last sleep, or even of how he came to exist. More isolated than any other vampire, Weyland is not lonely, for as a pure predator he is complete unto himself, indifferent to the humans who are his prey. The vampire's sexual magnetism is real, but it's simply a hunting lure: he has no sexual interest in people, though he can feign it well enough to seduce his victim. In this, he makes no distinction between men or women, for all are finally food to him. Indeed, he finds sex with humans unpleasant, much the way we would find having sex with an animal before we ate it repulsive. All Weyland lives for is to live; he is an animal with an intellect but no link to humans, no identification with them or, indeed with anything except his own predatory needs.

The Vampire Tapestry tells Weyland's tale through five short stories about his encounters with humans. In the first story an elderly woman suspects he is a vampire and, having prepared herself, shoots Weyland when he attacks her, forcing him to flee the college where, as an anthropology instructor, he has been preying on the volunteers in his dream research lab. This story is not really about Weyland, though it provides much information about vampires, and its themes become important in Weyland's story later on. In the second story, a young boy named Mark protects Weyland from exploitation by his uncle and his Satanist friend, who find Weyland wounded and in flight. They try to turn him into a sideshow attraction and, convinced that he is a supernatural being, intend to torture him into giving up his magical secrets before killing him. Mark establishes a kind of friendship with Weyland, who spares his life after killing his wretched uncle.

In the third story, Weyland visits a psychologist, Dr. Floria Landauer, who initially thinks she has a particularly fascinating madman, equal to Freud's Wolfman, on her hands. Slowly Floria realizes that Weyland really is a vampire, and in dealing with this dangerous, exotic predator, she becomes attracted to him as the focus of the anxiety, loss, and fear that pervade her own life due to the recent death of her mother and the breakup of her marriage. When Weyland decides to run away, he comes to Floria's apartment to kill her and erase all trace of what she knows about him, but she promises she will not reveal his identity. They consummate their bargain in more ways than one by having sex, which releases Floria from her own fears, while it touches Weyland in a strange and disturbing way he cannot explain.

In the fourth story Weyland goes to New Mexico to join another university faculty. There, during a performance of *Tosca*, he becomes overwhelmingly excited by the representation of violence, desire, and cruelty he sees in Scarpia. Maddened, he bolts from the hall and kills a young tenor, unable to explain why he has responded in such a way to music and drama. In the final story, Weyland must confront both the Satanist who has pursued him from New York and the death of a colleague, Irv, who commits suicide. Weyland is unable to recognize the open and passionate Irv's dire emotional situation or respond to his desire to talk about it, nor can he fully grasp the grief Irv's real friends feel at his loss. Moved by the desire to go into hibernation, "Weyland" realizes why he can never recall his past lives when he reawakens. As a predator he must remain detached from his prey, but in living among humans he forms relationships with them, comes to care about them, and finds himself beginning to empathize with them. Such feelings are a debilitating disease to a predator, so he must lose his memory and his connection to humanity during his long sleep in order to hunt without inhibition upon waking.

Before he sleeps, Weyland experiences an intense wave of memory, the "joy and ache" of which allows him a moment of the connection with humanity he has "gathered in his 'Weyland' existence." But Weyland is not disturbed by his final realization of why he is conditioned toward detachment; indeed, he welcomes sleep, as his increasing sense of empathy and connection to humans is dangerous and ultimately somewhat unpleasant to him. If he did not sleep he would become like Barnabas or Louis, a self-divided being whose nature wars against itself. Charnas's book is dispassionate in tone; we are not compelled to identify with Weyland; indeed, only the last two stories are told even partly from his point of view, and these narrate his confusion at the fundamental human experiences of identification with art and with the suffering of others. This vampire is neither a superior being nor, really, an inferior one.

Weyland's story is in itself a fascinating exploration of the nature of the predator, but in the context of the vampire story, it functions as a critique of the romantic vampire or, indeed, any use of the vampire as a figure of humanity. While Weyland is neither evil nor degraded as is Herzog's Dracula, he is relentlessly alien. Human in form, he is psychologically completely unlike human beings. Weyland defines the difference between vampires and humans by the fact that he is a pure predator and we are not; our capacity for empathy, which allows us to form relationships and to represent ourselves through art, is simply beyond him—except for that one small moment before he sleeps. Indeed, while the final story of *The Vampire Tapestry* has a melancholy quality for the reader, quite the opposite is true for Weyland. Our desire that he would be able to overcome his predatory nature and accept his relationships with humans is the exact opposite of what he wants. If we see his retreat into hibernation as a loss, he finds it a relief.

Thus the vampire illuminates our nature, and Weyland represents the failure of pure nature as a basis for the human; there is no basis for humanity other than what we define in our social connections. Such a radical naturalization of the vampire story, in which romance, moral and psychological torment, and art surround the vampire but either make no impression on him or present an incomprehensible distraction, makes the vampire into the image of what we fear becoming: an animal with an intellect. In this, Charnas affirms the same values as Yarbro—art, tolerance, love, and reason—but embodies in the vampire not the antithesis of such ideals but the utter lack of them. Yarbro's Savonarola is perverse, while Weyland is not only natural, he in some sense *is* nature. By depriving Weyland of the guilt and intense self-awareness of Rice's vampires, Charnas presents an image of the vampire starker than any of the gorgeous fiends. Weyland hasn't even the "love of damnation," for he is incapable of loving anything. Even his identification with Scarpia, that sudden moment when art holds the mirror up to one's face, produces in him not self-realization but the overwhelming need to kill.

Though *The Vampire Tapestry* may have its origins primarily in exploring a new way of imagining the vampire story—as a sophisticated artistic experiment that converts a story of the supernatural into science fiction—it functions as a post-human vampire tale precisely because it severs all links with the Gothic, the supernatural, and the nineteenth century. Weyland, who has no past, is the man of the future; it is he who will awaken in a hundred years to find a new kind of society after all the people he has known during his last life are dead. Since he is a unique mutation, Weyland is not the apocalyptic harbinger of a new species; but in the context of the vampire stories of the late 1970s and early 1980s, *The Vampire Tapestry* does introduce a vampire representing a new kind of danger, a being who cannot be integrated into the human world because, as he is continuously losing his past, he is always losing his humanity. Though Herzog uses the traditions of the vampire story and the nineteenth century, while Charnas makes a radical break from them, both Harker and Weyland are the terrifying "new men" of a post-human future.

"It appears to be consuming your blood"

Whitley Strieber's novel *The Hunger* (1981) is in one sense a retelling of "Carmilla" as it involves the "seduction" of scientist Sarah Roberts by the vampire Miriam. It is also a story of a post-human gorgeous fiend, for the ancient Miriam is an endless sea of hunger—for blood, for sleep, for immortality, for eternal love. In her need for complete gratification, Strieber's vampire is the image of the post-human narcissist stripped of all empathy. Though Miriam has memories back to ancient Egypt, this vampire is not a creature of the past but a thoroughly modern being. Miriam lives in a continuous present bounded by sleep and hunger; she has hardly any recollections of her own past except for fleeting wisps of memory. The objects of art in her apartment are beautiful but disconnected from their social, historical, and human meaning; for Miriam, art, like her lovers, exists only to enhance her stylish, aesthetic existence.

Miriam is a predator, but unlike Weyland, she must have relationships with at least some of her prey, making selected ones her companions. Like Carmilla, Miriam loves her companions, but this love is only another form of her boundless need, for she consumes them too, just more slowly than ordinary prey. When Miriam tells her vampire lovers they will be together forever, she fails to tell them that they will remain young for only about two hundred years, then they shall age but not die, as did Tithonus in Tennyson's poem, which Strieber uses as an epigraph for the novel. Miriam keeps all who reach this state in coffins in the attic, where their bodies rot even as their minds remain active.

Though very different from the vampire, the humans in this story seek the same thing—immortality. Sarah Roberts, Miriam's target, and her husband Tom are scientists working on a project to slow the aging process through transforming blood; during experiments, they realize that monkeys infected with a certain virus may become immortal but also become vicious predators, devouring each other, and it is on this paradox their research is stuck. Sarah meets Miriam when John, Miriam's current companion, comes to the scientist in a hopeless attempt to reverse his sudden aging. Sarah finds Miriam attractive (a monster in the original definition of the term, she says, "a fabulous thing of the gods") because of Miriam's telepathic manipulation. In bringing Sarah over, Miriam forces her to murder Tom; Sarah then realizes Miriam is actually a vampire, a monster who literally stinks of death, and refuses to allow herself to be brought over. She immediately becomes one of the horrific mummies in the attic. But Sarah accepts her fate and finds peace in refusing to become a monster, in memories of love, and in faith that someday she and Tom will be reunited in a world beyond this life. The novel presents the triumph of the human over the vampire as the spiritual superiority of love over the animal need that drives Miriam. In retaining her humanity, Sarah achieves the kind of inner satisfaction that escapes Miriam, though at an extraordinarily high cost.

Though the final chapter returns to Miriam's point of view, Strieber makes it clear not only that Miriam is inferior to Sarah but that, in a moment of limited insight into her own situation, she recognizes it. "Miriam now realized that the gift she could confer was not above such a one as Sarah but beneath her. . . . No matter how her loneliness tempted her to find one who would last forever, she resolved never to attempt the transformation of another like Sarah, not this time, or the next time, or for all time." [2] Yet while Sarah affirms a value beyond Miriam's "beautiful" life, Strieber entwines that value with the horror of Sarah's corpselike existence, which may last millennia. If she does find "riches of peace and love that she had never known were there," it comes at the cost of seemingly unavoidable horror. Sarah's humanity becomes, in effect, superhuman and unimaginable, and we are left with the melancholy sense that Miriam is much closer to what we are than Sarah.

The 1983 film version of *The Hunger* changes the novel's story to make it even more grim. The film, Tony Scott's first, is characterized by a careful denaturalization of its world. Most of the action takes place either in Miriam's elaborate New York apartment or in Sarah's laboratory. The scenes in the apartment are ethereal, glowing with a warm, dusky light; they look like fashion advertisements for vampirism, a fitting appearance since Miriam lives the kind of life that exists only in such visionary materialism. In contrast, the lab scenes are harsh and ugly; the rare outdoor scenes only serve to remind us that there is a natural world outside science and vampirism (though this natural world is New York City).

In the movie Miriam is much the same as in the novel, but rather than "killing" herself, she is driven by Sarah into the arms of her corpselike former lovers, who destroy her. Sarah turns into a vampire in spite of herself, and the movie ends with her and her new companion together in yet another beautiful apartment, waiting for the Architectural Digest photographers, living an aesthetically charmed existence. While the novel emphasizes the superiority, however rarefied, of the human over the vampire, the movie focuses on the inevitability of the vampire; once one is infected, nothing can stop the hunger.

Despite the fact that these vampires are monsters, the film makes the sexual and aesthetic attractions of the vampires part of its visual appeal. Casting Catherine Deneuve as Miriam and David Bowie as the decaying John merges the vampire with real-life celebrity (Bowie is not Byron, but he will do), anticipating Lestat and Timmy Valentine, the later rock star vampires. The world of the vampires has a mysterious beauty that lingers even as horror increases. It's hard not to look at Sarah's apartment in the final shot and think, "that would be a beautiful place to live," even though we have seen what the vampires really are. In advertising the movie's release, MGM certainly exploited the sensationalism of the love scenes between Deneuve and Susan Sarandon, who played Sarah. With their aspirations to celebrity and fashionable beauty—in contrast with the tormented psyche of Louis or Barnabas—Miriam and John represent the post-human vampire as the embodiment of contemporary human aspirations.

While Strieber's novel overtly affirms the superiority of humanity despite Miriam's survival, the movie makes it clear that the vampire, in one form or another, is the only true victor. Though the vampires are monsters, the movie offers us no alternatives; Sarah is doomed once her blood is infected, even if she is momentarily Miriam's slayer. Though *The Hunger* may caution against vampires by deeming their immortality ultimately delusive and their love empty, it also foresees the undead as our inevitable fate. The vampire is already in our blood, whether we know it or not.

"There is no magic"

While George Romero's *Martin* (1976) has neither gorgeous fiends nor imperious Lords of the Undead, the movie offers remarkable insight into the vampire's significance for us. At the very moment when Rice's romantic undead celebrities defined the vampire for most of America, *Martin* presented the vampire's predatory compulsion as an image of contemporary spiritual emptiness and pathology. Martin the "vampire" says over and over that "there is no magic," meaning that he has no supernatural powers, but also that being a vampire is only an extreme form of freakishness in a world that has no values of any kind. Martin, a severely disturbed young man, is in fact a serial killer but believes he is an eighty-four-year-old vampire. He attacks women, drugs them, then slits their wrists to drink their blood, making it appear as if they have committed suicide. The scenes of his attacks, particularly the one that takes up the first ten minutes of the movie, are quite graphic and horrible; the victim's terror, not Martin's desire, is the object of our identification. Martin kills out of need, a drive that is deformed by his own fear and inadequacy rather than titanic desire. Martin is pathetic, a confused, weak young man who has become a vampire because he cannot find a way to be a human being.

Martin has improvised an identity out of family legends (his Uncle Cuda has a photograph album of other family members who were "cursed"), B movies, and his own sickness. Periodically the movie cuts to black-and-white scenes of earlier days in "the old country," when a romantic Martin in a cape killed a young woman and was chased by a mob; the sequences are actually Martin imagining himself in a Universal Studios horror movie, as the scenes mix elements of the 1930s *Dracula* and *Frankenstein*. Throughout the movie he complains that it is so difficult to accomplish in real life what movie vampires do effortlessly. He would rather be a fictional character than a real person, but his only insight into his condition is that he is so unlike his chosen models.

Though we can't forget the horror of Martin's murders, we come to see that he is sick and would prefer to be normal. The older members of his family, who also believe he is a vampire, have sent him from Philadelphia to Braddock, a dying steel town outside of Pittsburgh. Uncle Cuda, who is from "the old country," takes the notion that Martin is a vampire completely seriously, but Cuda's idea of vampires is an amalgam of folklore and popular movies, which makes him unable to understand what Martin really is. Cuda wants to be Van Helsing, but Romero's vampire, disassociated from both folklore and popular culture, is a symptom of a world that needs to imagine vampires as romantic creatures for which no Van Helsing will suffice. At one point Martin dresses up in the Lugosi costume and scares his uncle, who cowers in fear as his nephew walks away laughing. To a degree Romero laughs at us as well, because this scene of fog and menace gives us the vampire moment we expect, perhaps even hope for, to make a movie the magical escape we recall from Hammer and Universal. But that is just a game; Martin's life is serious.

Post-Human Vampires: "We Are Animals"

Martin becomes friends with his cousin Ginger while living with Uncle Cuda, which is as close as Martin comes to a normal relationship with anyone; though the audience is always worried that he will attack her. While she realizes he is strange, she has no way to gauge the depth of his sickness and recognizes in him a fellow sufferer under Uncle Cuda's traditionalist tyranny. Though Ginger and Martin are often allies against Cuda, there is no liberation from the ossified past, only desultory moving on, as Ginger finally leaves town with her worthless boyfriend to escape the stultification of Braddock and her Uncle's home. Martin's only other approach to normality is an affair (his first experience of "sexy stuff" with a woman who is awake and alive) with a clinically depressed housewife, Mrs. Santilli, who eventually commits suicide. Hearing of Mrs. Santilli's death, Uncle Cuda, who knows Martin has been doing odd jobs for her, thinks he has killed her and drives a stake into his heart; there the movie ends, with Martin executed for the one murder he didn't commit.

Unlike Rice's Louis, Martin is too bizarre and unself-aware to be more than an object of pity. The psychotic adolescent can't really figure out what is going on (he never realizes that Mrs. Santilli is depressed), making the fantasy of the vampire his only explanation for who and what he is. Like Herzog's Dracula and Harker, Martin is a figure of sickness in a world that has become sick. Braddock is a town in collapse; there is no work and the streets are no longer safe, as we see punks hassling women in the supermarket parking lot. Religion has failed; the church has burned down and the new priest, played by Romero, is more interested in wine tasting than faith or the condition of his parishioners. Cuda's belief in the old ways is a joke; neither crosses nor garlic bother Martin, and he can't be exorcised. Martin spends most of his nights on the phone to a radio talk show and becomes a mock celebrity known as "the Count" in trying to explain his situation to the host, who effectively becomes his confessor. After Martin is staked, a victim of Cuda's obsession with the supernatural, the movie leaves a bleak sense of an empty and pointless world from which escape is impossible, even escape through fantasy.

Such themes are hardly novel; people living marginal lives in rust belt towns, women failed by men, and depressed old people living in the past are the stuff of the contemporary realism in the work of Bobbie Ann Mason, Russell Banks, and Raymond Carver. But organizing these themes around the vampire story gives them a metaphoric quality that takes them out of psychological or sociological realism. The failure of magic, the loss of the past, of hope, of possibility are all focused through the figure of the vampire, which reflects our empty attempts to re-enchant a broken reality. The horror of Martin's crimes contrasts with his own emptiness; he has become a vampire because it at least gives him a name and an identity in a world in which these things are lost. Romero's film demonstrates how a nostalgic fantasy, the romantic vampire, allows us to avoid the present realities of social decay and moral emptiness. Martin is, though in no way he understands, correct in saying he is a vampire, for he is what the vampire becomes in the contemporary world: the image of our loss of human identity.

Martin, like *Blood for Dracula,* is a "last vampire" movie about how Count Dracula has become obsolete and is, for Romero, a figure better suited to define the pathology of our time than Good and Evil, or romance and desire. What Martin does in his deranged psyche, Romero has done with the movie by remaking the vampire legend into a contemporary tale with a completely new meaning. Of course, like Morrissey, Romero doesn't really expect vampire movies to stop being made, rather he uses the vampire to take a harder look at the decay our fantasy life, its disconnection from reality. While Romero, who is from Pittsburgh, locates his sense of decay in a very specific moment in the rust belt of the mid-1970s, his perception of the disconnection between popular fantasy life, tradition, faith in a meaningful future, and religion goes beyond this locale. The inadequacy of such fantasies as the vampire—which of course Rice finds perfectly and beautifully adequate—is part of the disintegration of cultural fabric and humanity in Romero's movie.

"I'm a vampire! I'm a vampire!"

Robert Bierman's *Vampire's Kiss* follows Romero's lead to the extent that it too is both a satire of the "cult" of the romantic, erotic vampire and a critique of the post-human future. *Vampire's Kiss* uses the same essential plot as *Martin*—a young man commits crimes thinking he is a vampire—but shifts the setting to yuppie New York in the 1980s. The vampire makes a perfect symbol for the empty inner life of the soulless yuppie of the late twentieth century. *Vampire's Kiss* invokes the same kind of emptiness shown in *Martin,* though New York is far more attractive than Braddock, in a Studio 54 sort of way; vampires still like discos eight years after Hamilton first tasted the night life. This is emptiness in the midst of plenty rather than in the midst of decay, a future that looks bright but has no real value. *Vampire's Kiss* shares motifs with Jay McInerney's *Bright Lights, Big City* and Brent Easton Ellis's *American Psycho,* but it is also a cautionary tale of the post-human future as well as one about present-day life in the Big Apple.

Peter Loew, played by Nicholas Cage, is a psychotic literary agent who is in therapy when the story begins; he belongs there, for he is a disgusting, egocentric predator before he ever becomes a vampire. Snobbish and deeply self-involved, he takes pleasure in terrorizing his secretary, Alva (Maria Conchita Alonso), by verbally abusing her, making her hunt through hundreds of files for a lost contract no one needs, and finally, in the grip of his "vampirism," raping her. Even when he doesn't think he's a vampire, it is virtually impossible to sympathize—let alone identify—with Peter. The movie initially allows a slight possibility that it is a "real" vampire story; a bat flies into Peter's apartment; later, we see scenes of a woman named Rachel with sizable incisors biting him and sucking his blood, though we also see scenes of Peter talking to her when she is manifestly not there. Peter wears a small Band-Aid on his neck where the fang marks would be, so we never see them when Rachel isn't around. However, Peter is watching Murnau's *Nosferatu* on television while Rachel bites him, and later he begins walking with Orlock's stoop-shoulder gait; as with Martin, Peter creates an identity for himself out of the fantasies from the past and then acts accordingly.

Everything Peter does that makes him think he's a vampire we see as a grotesque joke. He says he can't see himself in the mirror, but it's quite clear to the audience that he does cast a reflection. He tries to shoot himself after raping Alva, but as she only wants to scare him, her gun is loaded with blanks; he concludes that he's immortal. Peter buys a set of false vampire teeth (plastic rather than the expensive fiberglass ones, as he has run out of cash) and at a disco kills a young woman by biting through her carotid artery. Vampire Rachel appears to him and tells him he is worthless and disgusts her. When he runs into her on the dance floor and begins shouting that she's a vampire and has turned him into one, she looks like a perfectly normal person with regular size teeth; she knows his name, but doesn't seem to recall being his vampire/lover.

Whether Rachel is a vampire or not is immaterial, for Peter has not become a vampire, he's simply become a psychotic version of his own horrible self. This is clearly a kind of triumphant liberation for him; at one point he skips down the street shouting, "I'm a vampire, I'm a vampire, I'm a vampire," to the passersby, who take relatively little notice. Disillusioned about the pleasures of vampirism after being tossed out of the disco (his victim's body hasn't been discovered yet) he picks up a broken board and, telling people he's a vampire, asks them to kill him. The delusions intensify as he imagines a session with his psychologist—this scene is intercut with shots of Peter talking to a mailbox as the sun rises—in which she not only sets him up with another client with normal size teeth as a new lover but absolves him of rape and murder, assuring him that she will take care of the police. Meanwhile, Alva has told her brother Jaime that Peter raped her; Jaime goes to Peter's apartment armed with a tire iron. He finds Peter hiding under his inverted couch, which he uses instead of a coffin. Peter places the stake above his heart and Jaime jams it into his chest, killing him. The movie ends by returning to the opening shot of crepuscular New York.

The strangely compelling and repelling quality of the movie rests mostly on Nicholas Cage's performance. He said at the time of release that he played Peter as if he was Jerry Lewis, and this is as good a description as any. Not only is Peter repulsive in his acts, but his manner is bizarre and thoroughly artificial in three different styles: selfish creep, full-bore psychotic, and would-be vampire. Unlike Martin, who we come to understand better than he does himself, we never understand Peter, who has no psychological depth because he is simply an object of satire. Even in the grip of psychosis, this yuppie scum never seems a victim of anything except his own crabbed and miserable emptiness. We don't see Peter descend into pedatory behavior, for he has no good qualities to descend from; instead we observe him in the terminal stages of his disintegration, when being a vampire becomes the "logical" and, at first, exciting thing to be.

The movie, which was billed as a comedy when it was released, has two main objects of comic satire. On one hand, the yuppie with his self-indulgent, vicious egotism is the obvious target. There is also a racial subtext; Peter is white; Jackie, his first girlfriend, and Rachel the vampire/lover are both well-off, light-skinned African Americans; while Alva is a working-class Latina. The film implies an equation that follows each step in his devolution: rich white yuppie = psycho = vampire. But the idealization of the vampire is also a target here. In *Martin,* the vampire is a folklore figure and a pop-culture image that Martin uses to concoct an identity, which he can't find anywhere else. Martin imagines himself a romantic, nineteenth-century-style vampire with a cape, while Peter allows himself to be possessed by Murnau's troll.

In *Vampire's Kiss,* the vampire is the product of an impoverished imagination that has lost all ethical sense. While Martin is terrifying in his murders but sympathetic in his lost, hopeless quality, Peter is scary mostly because he's so disgusting. While we see that Martin needs treatment beyond what the radio host can offer, Peter's therapy is simply another one of his many indulgences, an accouterment of the yuppie lifestyle. In both movies the vampire plays a double role. On the one hand, it serves as the sign of the imaginative and spiritual emptiness of men who substitute the fantasy of the romantic vampire for their own identities. At the same time, though, Romero and Bierman renew the imaginative force of the vampire by making it into a figure of neither liberation nor evil, but of satire; the vampire functions not as a cultural icon, but as the icon of the failure of culture itself.

Urban Monsters, Spiritual Terror

Post-human vampires increasingly provide images of our essential inner emptiness and victimhood rather than images of pathology, such as Martin and Peter Loew, or of alien monsters like Miriam. By the 1990s, the post-human vampire is already here, already controlling us, and we can no longer rely on our own power to save us. In such works as *Habit, Unholy Hungers,* [3] and *The Addiction,* [4] the vampire's victim becomes the center of concern, because that victim is everyone. The underlying concern in *Habit* is not what a vampire is but what makes John, the central character, its prey. Some of John's vulnerability stems from the unresolved emotions raised by the death of his father, a loss that also symbolizes his state of disconnection from anything except his own needs; in this state, John has no capacity for self-restraint. John's vampire habit represents the need for excitement in the face of an empty world, a world in turn made empty by the heedless pursuit of stimulation. The post-human vampire is the reality of contemporary urban existence, and behind writer/director Larry Fessenden's story lies both the AIDS epidemic and drug use, the real-life deadly indulgences for which the vampire stands.

The story's impact turns on our recognition, virtually from the moment we see John's lover, that she is a vampire and that John should see this, too. Her behavior is too strange, the sexual relationship too disturbing, for him not to notice (after their first encounter she leaves him unconscious in a public park); yet he is oblivious to everything but his need for the thrills she offers. The movie is powered less by sympathy for John than a sense of frustrated horror as he plunges toward his death—except in the inescapable identification with his terror as the vampire pursues him in the final scenes. This is a slayerless world and nothing can stop the vampire, not crosses, not garlic, not stakes.

Barbara Hort's *Unholy Hungers: Encountering the Psychic Vampire in Ourselves and Others* (1996) is a Jungian, psychological self-help book that takes the post-human vampire as an archetype of human identity, and it too is about us as the vampire's prey.

> The beast hungers for survival but not for life as we know it, since life implies the warmth of a beating heart and the light of a shining soul. The beast has neither heart nor soul. It has only a clever mind and insatiable hunger. . . . So the beast must prey upon us, the living. . . . If we are lucky we merely die. If we are less fortunate . . . we will become the thing to which we have fallen prey, and we will be compelled to feed in the same parasitic way. Thus the feeding frenzy spreads. . . . The beast is ancient and global and growing. . . . We call the beast *vampire*.

While for Fessenden, the vampire is a monster of the urban world, Hort sees in the vampire an ancient psychic archetype, but both use the vampire as an image of the dire state of humanity, now and in the future. If the liberated vampire was partly inspired by the ideas of self-acceptance and self-affirmation from an earlier phase of the self-help movement, Hort specifically consigns both Lestat and Saint-Germain to the status of deadly monsters whose charisma is merely lure. But while John cannot be saved, Hort's book is all about how we can, in effect, become our own slayers; indeed, the book itself enacts a kind of vampire slaying by returning the vampire into a figure of unalloyed evil, "sneering and stalking, slavering and drooling." Our encounter with the vampire is still inescapable, though it may force us into contact with the divine; and so the perilous battle with creatures of the dark may begin to lead us to the light. These two versions of the post-human vampire story, the tale of urban emptiness and the story of spiritual combat, come together in Abel Ferrera's *The Addiction*.

"Tell me to go away"

The Addiction, directed by Abel Ferrera and written by Nicholas St. John, is a Catholic vampire movie; most of Ferrera's recent films, such as *Bad Lieutenant*, are rooted in a Catholic drama of sin and redemption. At the same time, Ferrera and St. John come to such work with a history of low-budget sensation movies such as *Ms. 45*, a woman's revenge fantasy, and *Slumber Party Massacre*, whose title needs no gloss. *The Addiction* begins with slides of My Lai and returns to photos of human carnage again and again, particularly the Nazi death camps; there are complementary shots of street life and the drug culture that inhabits it. Framed with these scenes, the vampire story becomes explicitly an allegory for the problem of accepting responsibility for ourselves in the face of human evil. Filmed in a luminous black and white, the movie's visual quality echoes its allegorical version of the vampire story. Throughout, Ferrera creates the sense that even in the deepest darkness there is light waiting to break free, the glow that needs only to be acknowledged; just as the addiction of vampirism may be overcome by accepting the illumination of the spiritual world.

As with *Habit, The Addiction* begins with the victim. Katherine Coughlin, a graduate philosophy student played by Lily Taylor, is taken suddenly and quickly by a vampire one night. The vampire challenges her to tell her to go away and really mean it, but Katherine can only plead with the vampire, repeating an ambiguous "please" (Please bite me? Please go away?). After she is bitten, the vampire sneeringly calls her a collaborator and leaves her to crawl home sick and wounded. The weakness that makes her vulnerable is ethical: she doesn't believe in evil and thus can't reject it.

Katherine quickly embraces being a vampire and makes spreading this curse her purpose. Her addiction to human blood, violence, and predation makes her studies in philosophy hollow and arid, but her descent into evil makes her more and more attuned to its existence in the world and, most strikingly, in herself. She meets an older, more experienced vampire (Christopher Walken), a gorgeous fiend who, after feeding on Kathy, tells her how he has learned to control his addiction and live as almost human, accepting his own degradation by making it the source of his strength—he lives to resist himself. This, he says, and Kathy comes to agree, is real freedom, the only kind humans can have.

Kathy continues to work on her dissertation, focusing on how philosophy is a search for not truth but power, an attempt to influence and control others, to make an impact on another ego. We are all thus collaborators with the vampire, only some have not yet been bitten and accepted this. She becomes confident and calm, assuming that she understands humanity and its inevitable cycle of descent into animal nature, which is what we resist, and yet that resistance becomes what we are. After passing her oral exam, she invites members of her department and their friends to a party where, alongside the vampires she has brought over and the woman who originally turned her, she plans to attack them. On her way home she passes a priest telling people that God loves them and handing out leaflets inviting them to attend church. She asks him to come with her—previously no one has been able to refuse—but he politely declines, explaining that he must continue his work. Though she cannot admit it, Kathy suddenly realizes that her theory is wrong, that humans do not have to surrender to mere human need, that we can say no to evil. Before the party she raves to herself, "I won't submit, I won't submit," meaning that she will not submit her carefully cultivated human will to God. She goes through with the attack at the party, which she ironically calls "sharing what I've learned."

The party massacre portrays the vampires as animals in a feeding frenzy. Kathy wanders from her apartment, glutted and dazed from the feeding; blood smears her face, soaks her dress, clots her hair. She collapses on the street and is taken to the hospital, where she accepts Christ and takes communion. Finally, Kathy transcends human needs; in the last shot, we see her in a serene, pale, light, looking down at a gravestone with her name on it, though she seems to be alive. She walks away from the grave, and the camera pans up to a statue of Jesus; after having descended into the darkness like an animal, she finally comes back to the light and realizes her spiritual existence.

The Addiction is a very severe movie, with little of the bitter, grotesque humor that permeates *Martin* and *Vampire's Kiss,* though for those who have been through it there is something grimly comic about writing a dissertation. On the other hand, not many vampire movies quote Feuerbach seriously (or comically, for that matter). Ferrera and St. John take the risk of linking the vampire story to tales of real human atrocity, such as the Holocaust and My Lai, and insist on making the viewer think about the meaning behind the vampire. *The Addiction* is as much a moralist's tale of redemption as *Bram Stoker's Dracula,* but while Coppola accepts human love as the road to salvation, St. John and Ferrera assert that only by coming to Christ can one be saved.

The Addiction is the fullest elaboration of the vampire as the feral intellect, for these vampires are both animals and intellectuals. The predatory animal in humans involves not simply the hunger, the needs of the flesh, but the intellect, the arrogance and pride that assume we can reason our way to ethical understanding unaided b sprituality, when in fact all we can do is repeat a hopeless cycle of degradation. The vampire, who seeks never to die, can never die into Christ and be saved and thus can never feel love. The vampire, like the philosopher, is an image of humanity lost in its own needs and ego, whether those needs are of the body or the mind. *The Addiction* is probably the starkest acceptance of the vampire as an image of humanity, but it is also the most rigorous in insisting on the need to turn away from mere humanity to a spiritual power.

Of course, Ferrera and St. John's story, like Hort's, "works" only if you already believe. [5] Indeed, it implicitly poses the question of whether we would rather believe in vampires or Christ's redeeming love; clearly Ferrera thinks we'd rather believe in vampires. The vision of the emptiness of secular rationalism and its fantasy avatar in Walken's vampire, a nosferatu who has read too much Bataille, is powerfully conveyed, but the reality of a spiritual realm through which we can be redeemed appears only in the ambiguous final scenes of the movie. The quality of Katherine's resurrection is inexplicable, we can see that she has been saved ("cured"), but we don't know the movie's criteria for what that means. By turning to a traditional opposition to the vampire, the Catholic Church, Ferrera makes clear that if we accept the notion of the dark side and Evil, we will have to turn to the light and God to escape the abyss. The final paradox of the movie, though, is that it is through the vampire story that Ferrera can find a way to articulate these religious ideas in contemporary culture. What dominates our imagination is the imagery and narrative of the vampire, not the language and perspective of religion.

"But there is a better way to live"

The terror of the vampire in these post-human stories is not that they will come and get us in the night but that we are already exactly like them, needing, as with Katherine Coughlin, only the perfunctory bite to make us aware of our nature. If this was all they did, the post-human vampire story would be a horror story indeed, and part of their force lies in their articulation of our fears about who we are and where we are going. But because they are also cautionary tales, the post-human vampire stories express the desire to affirm values and ideals beyond need, the longing for the humanity we are losing. The aspiration for some form of spiritual existence and the affirmation of love and family are clearly part of what humanity means here, but these things are often recognizable only as the absences made visible in the image of the vampire. At every turn, these works embody the awareness—or perhaps the fear—that such things may be every bit as fictitious as vampires. Only *The Addiction* is clear about what the better way to live might be, and this message is weakened by the fact that it is easier to delineate a forceful image of humanity in the post-human vampire than in the spirit who has come to Christ.

Though it is a nightmare of the future, the post-human vampire story is, in its way, nostalgic in its longing for a secure sense of the spiritual and ethical, for traditional human connections and community in the face of the post-human. Whether such an ideal of humanity was truly part of the past is as indeterminate as whether or not the Victorians were actually repressed. Like repression, tradition and nostalgia define our relations to the past, which, in the end, is how we understand our fears about the future.

5

THE DRACULA VARIATIONS: PART II

Though the vampire had never left the public eye entirely, the early 1990s saw an upsurge of interest in Dracula and Stoker. The accumulation of vampire stories over the previous twenty-five years had created a stream of continuing interest that needed the right conditions to be tapped. Stoker's novel also probably benefitted from the upsurge in interest in movies based on nineteenth-century novels of all kinds, so *Dracula* joined the parade of works by Austen and James on the big screen. The oncoming anniversary of the publication of *Dracula* provided another catalyst and advertising hook; as the century ended, American culture had become obsessed with anniversaries and memorial observations of all kinds. Vampires returned to television because cable and new networks needed programming and had the ability to target specific markets. Video, then DVD, made earlier vampire movies readily available again. The publicity surrounding the production and release of Coppola's film, which boasted a major director and major studio, with well known stars—Anthony Hopkins, Keanu Reeves, Winona Ryder, and Gary Oldman—pushed the vampire back into general public notice. As always, vampires make more vampires.

While Coppola's *Bram Stoker's Dracula* made a complex attempt to remain faithful to the novel, other writers, in the relative explosion of vampire stories in the 1990s, began to use Dracula as a figure through which to imagine our future. In these works, many of the motifs and characters of

Stoker's novel reappear, the Count returns to his role as monster, and his human opponents once again become the focus of our attention. But while *Dracula*'s imaginative power seems strong in its many offspring, they are clearly moving further and further away from their source; *Dracula* is no longer our story. This creates a kind of palimpsest effect, as we can recognize *Dracula* showing through at points in new works that are both parallel to and quite different from the original. Dracula himself is more frequently a symbolic presence in the early-1990s stories, brooding over our future, an image and symbol rather than a character.

Kim Newman's *Anno Dracula* (1992), Dan Simmons's *Children of the Night* (1992), Marie Kiraly's *Mina* (1994), Roderick Anscombe's *The Secret Life of Lazlo, Count Dracula* (1994), and Michael Almereyda's *Nadja* (1994) [1] don't pretend fidelity to Stoker's *Dracula;* they tell the "real" story, the "untold" story, or the post-Dracula story. *Anno Dracula* is postmodern counterhistory, *Children of the Night* melds elements of horror and science fiction with a post–cold war adventure novel, *The Secret Life* blends the true crime story with the case history, *Mina* is a feminist novel of woman's liberation, and *Nadja* is a postmodern story of reconciliation. Finally, *Dracula: A Norton Critical Edition* (1997), edited by Nina Auerbach and David J. Skal, simultaneously remains utterly faithful to Stoker's original while revising it by literally binding it to a collection of critical rereadings in the liberationist line.

What Did Stoker Know of Vampires?

In *Children of the Night* (1992) Dan Simmons uses *Dracula* as *JFK* uses the Warren Report. While *Dracula* may be the "official" story of the vampire, in *Children of the Night* we get the "real" story (lone gunman, ha!) straight from the historical Dracula, Vlad "The Impaler" Tepes himself, who actually is a vampire though not in any way Stoker would recognize. "I have read Stoker. I read his silly novel when it was first published in 1897 and saw the first stage production in London. Thirty-three years later I watched that bumbling Hungarian ham his way through one of the most inept motion pictures I have ever had the misfortune to attend. Yes I have read and seen Stoker's abominable, awkwardly written melodrama, that compendium of confusions which did nothing but blacken and trivialize the noble name of Dracula." Simmons's Dracula is a ruthless warrior and politician whose power lies in his ability to leave behind the old ways in favor of the technology of the future. In *Children of the Night,* the vampire is not a metaphor for the future; he is the future, the secret power controlling it. *Children of the Night* takes place in the midst of contemporary geopolitics and medical research, at the end of cold war and the beginning of a new millennium, with an apocalyptic vampire conspiracy and a disturbingly corporate Count as the images of the new world order.

Vlad himself is a marginal character in the novel; while he narrates the first six chapters, he takes little part in the action until the end, nor does he have the intimate relationship with the Mina character, Dr. Kate Neuman, typical of other works that revise Stoker's novel. Neuman is an NIH doctor working with orphaned children in Romania (thousands of children were found virtually imprisoned in orphanages shortly after the fall of the Ceausesceu regime). She discovers one infant with a peculiar, deadly blood disease she can't identify. With the help of Father Michael O'Rourke (who first appeared as a child in Simmons's earlier novel *Summer of Night*) she smuggles the baby, whom she names Joshua, to the U.S. Neuman discovers that when Joshua ingests blood, his body renews itself; his genetics may hold the cure for cancer and AIDS, and the key to immortality.

Joshua is one of Vlad's offspring, and the condition he has is what made Vlad and others into vampires. The vampires have been the secret power behind the Ceausesceu government, and they send a team of agents to retrieve the child who kill Kate's ex-husband and graduate assistant/ nanny in the process. Shattered by their deaths and the loss of the child, Kate nonetheless returns to Romania to find Joshua. She and O'Rourke fall in love, recover emotionally, and escape with Joshua, snatching him away from a gathering of vampires on a mountaintop after learning about The Family (as the vampires call themselves) and their conspiracy to control the world.

As an adventure novel *Children of the Night* is extraordinarily successful. The action is swift and convincing, Neuman is a thoroughly appealing hero and O'Rourke an attractive lover/sidekick. Kate's dedication to Joshua is so uncompromising that she becomes a hero by replacing the slayer's violence with the medical and maternal power of healing. Neuman, mother and doctor, succeeds in a way that heroines of romantic vampire stories can't, for as her heroism doesn't grow out of a passion for Dracula but from her own core of values, she is finally able to extricate herself from the terror of the vampire. Despite Vlad's rejection of Stoker, Kate's story ends with the ideal of the family with which *Dracula* also concludes; although, with a professional woman, an ex-priest, and an adopted child, the family is throughly reconfigured for the contemporary reader. But at the same time, as she is no slayer, she leaves Dracula to do what he wants with the twenty-first century.

The novel is more complex than its straightforward, heroic adventure narrative, though. Interspersed throughout Kate's story are Vlad the Impaler's dreams and memories of his past life; we know Vlad's thoughts and history but Kate and Michael never do. We diverge from the heroes at the end, for, by reading Vlad's final monologue, we understand more about their situation than they do. The Family has divided into warring factions, traditionalists (blood drinkers) and modernists (who want to stay alive through injections of the serum Kate has used to cure Joshua), and Vlad has allowed Kate's escape with Michael and Joshua to meet his own ends. Kate and Michael may succeed, but they never get to the heart of what is actually going on. "I have thought about the child of mine who was taken that night. At first I considered retrieving him, of raising him the way I raised Vlad and Mihnea. But then I remembered what potential he holds and I have decided to let the woman doctor raise him and learn from him."

Vlad Dracul Tepes, who was living as American millionaire Vernon Deacon Trent, has returned to his native land and stopped drinking blood, and as he waits to die, he recalls his true history. The immortality and the blood drinking now have scientific explanations. Vlad's story is the monstrous and bloody tale of fourteenth-century Transylvanian realpolitik, the horrors of which now haunt him as bad dreams. Added to the events of Tepes's history is the ritual of blood drinking, which, while necessary to keep the members of The Family alive, is not only monstrous in itself but creates the predatory rage of the vampires. Vlad clearly was made into a monster not simply by the ritual of blood drinking but by the brutality of fourteenth-century politics and warfare. He is sane in being perfectly adapted to the reality of his time and thus is a monstrous madman. At the end of the novel Vlad decides, given that his kind can now live in the modern world through science and technology without losing any of their power, that he will put off his death.

> I have been a source of terror to my people many times in my long life. I know now that I would have welcomed being a savior to my people. Perhaps, through this child . . . just perhaps.
>
> Meanwhile, I am considering returning to the States, or at least the civilized part of Europe, to be closer to he laboratories making my hemoglobin substitute. It occurred to me recently that Japan is a place I have never lived. It is an intriguing place, filled with the energy and business that is the lifeblood I feed on now.
>
> In the meantime, I have given up thoughts of dying soon. Such thoughts were the products of illness, age, and bad dreams. I no longer have the bad dreams.
>
> Perhaps I will live forever.

We can read the ending of the novel optimistically, as Vlad's final meditation suggesting that as he leaves behind his bloody medieval heritage he is ready to become something beneficial for the world. The fantasy of being a savior is clearly pleasant for him and certainly better for would-be recipients of impaling; the end of the "bad dreams" seems to signal a kinder, gentler Dracula. Insofar as this is science fiction, the triumph of technology and science could be imagined to bring about a new golden age. Further, the novel's ending is fully within a traditional Christian symbology: God the father (Dracula) sends his son (Joshua) to save humanity; Kate, doctor of the body, Michael, doctor of the soul, and Joshua form a version of the Holy Family of Jesus, Mary, and Joseph. The blood offers life, perhaps immortality, for the human race.

But Vlad is not God, though he may aspire to this status, and he remains motivated by the political values of power and control. He desires not that Joshua learn from Kate and O'Rourke the lessons of love, devotion, and caring but that Kate learn the secrets of the child's body. Able to drop the medieval ritual and trappings of his family history, Vlad emerges into the twenty-first century with the power of money, science, and secrecy. He has a better chance of taking over the world through these means than Stoker's Count ever had by biting one throat at a time. As Kate,

O'Rourke, and Joshua escape via helicopter from the mountain where Dracula has massacred the members of The Family who oppose him, they look down on the clouds reflecting the stars: "The cloud tops gleamed beneath them as far as she could see in each direction. There was no sense now of national boundaries or of nations, of the darkness that lay below those clouds. Kate would not mind staying above these clouds for a while. She rocked the baby, crooning very softly, and watched out the window as they leveled off and flew northwest." Simmons suspends his heroic/holy family, his contemporary Mina and Van Helsing, above a dark world full of the ambiguous plans and power of a Dracula whose role in their lives they never fully grasp; they do not defeat the vampires, they escape them. Our lives may be ours, but the world is run by others; whether they decide to be our saviors or tormentors is a matter of their interests and needs, not ours.

Even vampires change with the times; from the medieval Family that works its will through violence and terror, they become a modern corporation that feeds on the lifeblood of capital and invention. The vampire becomes like capital itself—secret, mobile, and immortal. Though the novel is primarily science fiction, its elements of horror are significant since in horror stories knowledge and power are always dangerous. In *Children of the Night,* conspiracy and paranoia are the new world order. The novel envisions a split between the personal realm, in which love, family, and caring are paramount, and the ambiguous realm of history, the province of the vampire where only power matters. Kate realizes this; her desire to remain above the clouds is her recognition that on earth there isn't such peace. Perhaps most disturbing is that the novel does not allow us to resolve whether the optimistic or apocalyptic reading is right; only the unreadable future will make that clear.

"Now this Dracula has his *Bradshaw* by heart and calls himself 'modern'"

While *Children of the Night* looks remorselessly into the future by affirming the value of its untraditional traditional family, Kim Newman's *Anno Dracula* (1992) recreates the Victorian world as an unsettling and chaotic vision of the future. The novel accepts the inevitability of the post-human but forsees it approaching as a complex and difficult transformation in which the past, present, and future will coexist in a new world. Newman rewrites *Dracula* by rewriting the whole Victorian world through an alternative history that makes the late nineteenth century an image of the late twentieth. *Anno Dracula*[2] fuses metafiction with supernatural historical fantasy, shaping the imaginary past into an image of the real present, both made of equal parts of fiction and reality. *Anno Dracula* bears a family resemblance to novels such as E.L. Doctorow's historical pastiche, *Ragtime*, or Don DeLillo's Kennedy assassination fantasy, *Libra*; or, in another key, the Los Angles novels of James Ellroy, which interweave history with fiction, or Bruce Sterling's *The Difference Engine*, another reconstruction of the nineteenth century. It isn't possible to say that Newman's novel is "serious" or "comic"; such labels are irrelevant in the context of his self-consciously postmodern playing with literature and history. The vampire novel serves Newman's affirmation that it's as important that we imagine history as it is that we know it.

Anno Dracula imagines what would have happened if Mina, Van Helsing, and the rest had failed to destroy the Count. Van Helsing's head rests on a pike in front of the Tower of London; Quincey Morris and Jonathan Harker are dead; Mina, now a vampire, is Dracula's unwilling servant; Lord Goldaming has gone over to the vampires; and Dr. Seward, driven mad by the death of Lucy, stalks vampire prostitutes as the Silver Knife Killer, the novel's version of Jack the Ripper. Not only do vampires and humans coexist, but fictional characters and real people do as well. Oscar Wilde, Florence Stoker, and Cardinal Newman are in the novel, as is Merrick the Elephant Man. Lord Ruthven from Polidori's "The Vampyre" is prime minister, while Mycroft Holmes heads a secret cabal that manages England's empire from the Diogenes Club. Daniel Dravot from Kipling's "The Man Who Would Be King" is a vampire and the silent enforcer of this imperial junta. Doctors Henry Jekyll and Moreau conduct bizarre, sadistic medical experiments. "Future vampires" are also present; "the upstart Collins," "the buffoon Barlow," and "the hand-kissing Saint-Germain" are all mentioned in a brief diatribe by Ruthven on the woeful lack of vampire leadership. Count Orlock, so grotesque that even the vampires are repelled by him, is warder of the Tower of London. And these are only the tip of the iceberg among the allusions to both literature and history.

The destruction of Stoker's heroes and narrative parallels what has happened to Dracula-ruled England in that all links with the past have been irreparably ruptured. Dracula, having married Queen Victoria and become Prince Consort (the exact details of the courtship are hazy, though presumably the promise of eternal life and youth had their appeal even to the Widow of Windsor), has been in power for some time when the novel opens. The central character, Charles Beauregard, is in love with the beautiful vampire Genevieve Dieudonne, who is far older than Dracula, but cannot bring himself to come over to the undead. The story is a luridly extravagant tale of murder and conspiracy centered on Beauregard's involvement in the plot of True Blooded Englishmen (both vampire and human), which ends with Victoria's suicide forcing Dracula out of the palace.

The novel is based in part on a University of Sussex course on late Victorian revolt, which Newman cites in his afterword, directing our attention to fiction as a way of understanding history, to history as a way of understanding the present and future. When Newman imagines Dracula taking over England, he replaces nostalgic images of a serene Victorian empire with an incoherent and divided society much like a contemporary one. Dracula has brought swarms of vampires from their hiding places about Europe to live openly in Britain, and hustled the humans ("warms") who oppose him to concentration camps. England has become a thoroughly mixed society, riven with the plots and counterplots of strange alliances between vampires and warms. Warms can always choose to go over, but becoming a vampire is risky and not always a successful process; further, there are many different kinds of vampires, and some manage the transition better than others. The diversification among vampires, the mixture of vampires and humans creating a new society defined by difference, suggests the multicultural societies of the late–twentieth century, in which identity and nationality mix and flow across borders. Dracula and his horde of ancient, supernatural monsters are the harbingers of the new world, bringing inescapable change not simply in the order of society but in the nature of identity itself.

Dracula (who in his only appearance seems a cross between King Kong and Jabba the Hutt) is at his most evil ever, and we see what it would be like to live under the totalitarian reign of this monstrous egotist and his brutal minions. But there are also good and ambiguous vampires, just as there are bad warms, and it is difficult to draw clear lines between them. Though Dracula is driven out of England, the overthrow of this particular prince doesn't change England back to its "orderly" pre-Dracula state. Fighting an evil being is not the same as transforming a complex reality. As with every character in the novel, Beauregard finds himself living in an undefined and ambiguous new world, aware that Dracula is Evil in the classic sense, but also that Dracula has brought with him the world of the future.

Dracula's opponents are warms and vampires who cannot escape their own now-uncertain natures or their confusion over what their world is and who they are to become. They cannot hope to make sense of the world, and the choices this prematurely postmodern world of conspiracy offers are unsatisfying. Beauregard will forever be tempted to become a vampire, and we sense he will bring himself to do so. The meaning of this new, strange reality is forever hidden, and while it has its pleasures and temptations, to join it means accepting death—a literal risk—for an uncertain new form of life. For Newman, the contemporary world is not driven by opposition between humans and vampires so much as it is sodden with uncertainty, moving slowly and clumsily as humanity attempts to sort out its ideas about good and evil, truth and falsehood, under these new conditions.

Central to the novel's understanding of the contemporary situation is the failure of fact as a source of meaning. By mixing real and fictional characters, making the novel an imaginative recreation of the Victorian world as well as a version of *Dracula,* Newman affirms that imagination allows us to understand the world but only at the price of certainty about what is real and what is fantasy. While this allows us to grasp abstractions such as "history" and "society" in narrative form, the sense of efficacy and value we get is limited by the folding of the real into the imaginary. Just as we can never be sure we have spotted all the literary, historical, and vampiric allusions in *Anno Dracula,* once we accept the historical and social realms as imaginative creations in which fact and fiction are blurred, we can't get back to the real facts. Thus Dracula, who broods over the novel, does so as a fiction, the only thing around which we can order an incoherent reality.

"My brain has not fully woken to what I have done"

The Secret Life of Laszlo, Count Dracula (1994) by Roderick Anscombe, a psychiatrist with a specialization in schizophrenia and the psychology of murderers, was called by the *Baltimore Sun,* "Hannibal Lector by way of

Anne Rice," and there is some truth in this characterization. *The Secret Life* also recalls *Martin,* but without the grotesque humor or the pathos of Martin's situation. *The Secret Life* is Dracula's first-person account of his life as a late-nineteenth-century serial killer of young women; the title may invoke the infamous Victorian underground pornographic novel *My Secret Life.* The novel literally humanizes Dracula by fusing him with the serial killer, providing a "real" account of what lies behind the myth of Dracula. In doing so, though, Dracula becomes a terrifying embodiment of the post-human and the novel a story about the emptiness of mere fact as a source of meaning. Only our awareness of the Dracula of fiction can finally order this tale of madness and chaos.

    The Secret Life is in a sense the ultimate post-human vampire story: the vampire is presented as a figure of modernity through Laszlo, who is endowed with knowledge of medicine and a sense of the decadence of the late nineteenth century, which, as in *Anno Dracula,* stands in for the decadence of the late twentieth. Driven by the need to kill and mutilate, Anscombe's Count is searching for an impossible ultimate experience in his fusion of sexuality, pleasure, and violence. While the novel never suggests that Laszlo is anything but a monster, this view depends upon our own revulsion at his crimes and alienation from his warped sensibility, since the novel also works on the principle that we are fascinated with this character. The price of this technique is that, as we are never outside of Laszlo's perspective, Anscombe can never really present any compelling moral alternative to this monster within the novel. Because he is Dracula, Laszlo comes to stand for humanity in its rawest, most elemental state, posing the question, is this who we really are?

    Laszlo first discovered his need to kill and mutilate during his medical training in Paris. After seeing a young prostitute under hypnosis and then meeting her, he realizes that identity is mutable and uncertain, and in eventually killing her he brings a moment of stability to his own chaotic existence. Laszlo can write about his desires and his feelings but is incapable of understanding his nature; he can describe his own emptiness but not explore its meaning. He writes his journal less to understand his compulsions than to give himself the solidity his existence lacks. While as a natural rather than supernatural vampire he recalls Edward Weyland of *The Vampire Tapestry,* Weyland is simply biologically a different species than the humans who he kills for food. Laszlo, empty though he may be, is completely human and kills because he has no core identity. While he has the intense inwardness of Rice's vampires, Laszlo is unable to feel anything except a sense of disconnection from reality that is filled only by his horrific murders of young women. While he feels a faint revulsion toward his murders, he is in fact more intellectually curious, a doctor fruitlessly studying his own illness. His only attempt at salvation is to throw himself into Hungarian nationalism when he joins a conspiracy of aristocrats who want an independent Hungarian monarchy under Austrian Crown Prince Rudolph.

The essential premise of the novel is that we can understand the vampire and serial killer as two representations of the same state of human hollowness, the state of post-humanity. The insight that the vampire and the serial killer can symbolize the same ethical and psychological state is not new as such; Ted Bundy himself claimed vampirism. In Jonathan Demme's film *Silence of the Lambs,* the visual imagery surrounding Lector—his Gothic dungeon cell, his "travel suit" with a muzzle that makes him appear to have fangs, and of course graphic scenes of his cannibalism—evokes the vampire as the symbol behind this particularly melodramatic form of realism. Anscombe has pursued this metaphor to its logical conclusion and rewritten Dracula as the contemporary real-life monster.

When Laszlo is finally executed it is not for his real crimes as serial murderer. His childhood friend, a priest, when found with Laszlo's latest victim, is staked as a vampire by a crowd of maddened peasants and dies proclaiming the twentieth-century slogan "There is no God!" Laszlo is somewhat moved by the realization that his boyhood friend has died for him, but he cannot see how his actions have led the priest to enact the legend of the vampire for him, including denial of God and meaning. Laszlo's attempt to rescue his friend, his one decent act in the novel, leads to his own murder and the subsequent failure of the Hungarian nationalists' scheme. Ironically, Lazlo goes to his death hoping that his name will become meaningful as a symbol of patriotism and nationalism like his ancestors, pinning his hope for meaning on a cause he barely understands. It is of course the name of the monster and not the patriot that will live on.

While the tracing of the Count's pathology and its development across the decades is fascinating and precise, it is also empty, I think intentionally, because, like Laszlo, we cannot ever really come to understand his situation or his reasons for butchering young women. We may find an analytical explanation here, but in such matters fact alone fails. While the gorgeous fiend's self-awareness is grandiose and adolescent, Rice is after a larger form of consciousness; her novels are about a way of being in the world. However romantic and theatrical her fiends may be, they give the impression of wholeness, a truth that cannot be dissected the way Laszlo dissects his victims. Anscombe's translation of fantasy into realism ultimately embodies the emptiness of not only the serial killer but the very attempt to encompass the world through realism, for it produces understanding without meaning beyond the slim pathos embodied in Laszlo's ability to write about his compulsions yet not to learn anything.

The comparison with Lector is striking, for Thomas Harris's novels distinguish between the serial killers Francis Dolahyde and Jame Gumb, sick men who like Laszlo act out of compulsion, and Lector, who is a fantastical creature beyond human comprehension, the ultimate post-human vampire in all but name. Hannibal Lector, who despite his madness and feral intellect is able to read others with the most acute perception and insight, always conveys the sense of a meaningful truth at the heart of all human interchanges. Lector appears to possess knowledge and understanding that normal human beings lack, so encounters with him can have significance even while they are terrifying. While he is not a gorgeous fiend, Lector has a whole, if alien, vision of reality that none of the normal characters can achieve. Lector's understanding is, in the end, the insight of the predator into his prey's vulnerability, and like Edward Weyland, real connection to others or real understanding of his own nature is unnecessary. Lector's status as the most powerful representation of the serial killer in contemporary fiction rests on his links to the vampire, an aura of fantasy that creates meaning in a postmodern world where reality cannot. *The Secret Life* relies on the same afterimage of the fantastic: serial killers are meaningless deviants without the metaphor of the vampire to allow us to make sense of them.

"I still feel his blood in me. I still feel that passion his touch aroused"

In the same year that *The Secret Life* appeared, Marie Kiraly (the penname of Elaine Bergstrom) published *Mina,* which describes the events at the ending of *Dracula* from Mina's point of view, then goes on to tell of her life after the confrontation with Dracula. *Mina* is one of a series of novels Kiraly has written about the obscured heroines of nineteenth-century horror fiction, including *Elizabeth*, a rewriting of *Frankenstein*, and *Madelaine*, based on "The Fall of the House of Usher." In the foreword, Kiraly explains the impulse behind *Mina* and its relation to *Dracula*.

> In writing *Mina* I have tried to remain as faithful to the story of *Dracula* as possible. The novel *Dracula* is written as a series of first-person accounts by Van Helsing, Jonathan and Mina Harker and the others. Near the end of the story, Mina's first-person accounts are abandoned and her feelings about her ravishment by the vampire never described save by the men. Perhaps Stoker was uncomfortable dealing with the musings of the damned. Perhaps he was attempting to convey the notion that Mina was being lost to the men as Lucy had been earlier in the story. In any case, Mina's voice, so strong through the early part of the novel, is abruptly silent.
>
> I begin my novel here.
>
> While faithful to the original novel, I restore Mina to her rightful place in the final struggle with Dracula, then follow her back to London, and to the new struggle to move into the future with a memory that, like Bram Stoker's novel, and Dracula himself, can never really die.

The combination of fascination and frustration with Stoker, the desire to retain the link to the older novel, and the need to change it are equally strong. *Mina* embodies a double consciousness in a pastiche of a nineteenth-century work that allows us to discern the contemporary themes and point of view through the recreation of the past. This strategy may imply that the present is already there in the past, that it has simply not taken on its contemporary form, but it also suggests that the present can only be understood by remaking the symbols and stories of the past.

The unspoken reason for Stoker's imposition of silence on Mina is made clear in Kiraly's novel: he could describe neither her experience of pleasure and sexual discovery with Dracula nor her changing perceptions of the men around her. Of course, in a sense Mina exists only as Stoker imagined her, but Kiraly finds she cannot imagine Mina without imbuing her with a modern consciousness, one she assumes the reader will recognize as truthful—implicit but unrealized in Stoker's novel. Though Kiraly strives to portray Mina from within a nineteenth-century consciousness, she is also very aware that the whole point of rewriting *Dracula* is to make it contemporary, which *Mina* accomplishes by infusing it with the perspective of a modern woman. While *The Dracula Tape, Love at First Bite, Dracula* (1979), and *Bram Stoker's Dracula* recreate Mina through a romantic relationship with Dracula, Kiraly, like Simmons, is writing about escaping from Dracula, not through a return to traditional values but through the liberation of the self that comes with the liberation of sexuality.

Mina, as the maternal center of the band of vampire hunters, is far more restive in Kiraly's novel than she appears in *Dracula*. She sees John Seward as an egocentric fool and Van Helsing as dangerously righteous in his ruthless pursuit of vampires; though we also learn that he has lost his young wife and many friends to vampire attacks. Quincey Morris, on the other hand, turns out to be far more perceptive about Mina's situation than *Dracula* would lead us to think. *Mina* assumes that Dracula, powerful and malevolent, lives on in an immaterial state after he is beheaded, and the psychic link created when Mina drank his blood remains. As Dracula infected Mina with a latent vampirism as well as awakened her sexuality, the novel tells the story of her search to understand the relation between her sexual and vampiric impulses. Unable to explain her desires to her husband and caught in competition for his allegiance with his Aunt Millicent, who raised him and comes to live with them, Mina finds herself becoming more and more influenced by the vampire in her blood. While Mina genuinely loves Jonathan Harker, she begins an affair with the dissolute Lord Gance, whose pallid and gaunt appearance resembles a vampire's. With Gance she satisfies her desire for a full sexual life even though he isn't a vampire and she despises him.

As these events unfold, Mina also attempts to get translated the diary of one of Dracula's brides, the Countess Karina, who hates her vampire state yet cannot escape it. The search for a translator leads her to an encounter with two Romanian vampire hunters, who try to kill her when they realize that she has Dracula's blood in her veins and will become a vampire. Mina kills them both and in fact does find her taste for blood intensifying, so she introduces blood drinking into her increasingly disturbing sexual play with Gance. After Jonathan discovers the affair, Mina and Gance travel to Transylvania to find out if Dracula is still "alive." Gance, whose life is as empty and pointless as Laszlo's—though his vice is serial seduction rather than serial murder—goes to Dracula's castle and asks Illona, the leader of Dracula's brides, to make him a vampire. Instead, she uses his body to bring Dracula back to the material world.

To finally confront Dracula, Mina must resolve her relation to her own sexuality. The vampirism that infects her has clearly become entwined with her sexual desires; though she also recognizes that the desires and feelings Dracula allowed her to experience are morally different than vampirism, because vampirism is predatory as well as compulsive. Before she goes to Castle Dracula she persuades a particularly holy Orthodox monk to give her his blessing, which means that when Dracula (in the form of Gance) drinks her blood he effectively drinks the blood of Christ and so dies. Mina also allows Countess Karina, who has protected her from Illona, to drink her blood to release herself from vampiric imprisonment. Freed from the taint of vampirism, Mina resolves to return home, hoping that she and Jonathan can remain together, for she still loves him. Though she realizes that if he cannot accept what has happened and respond to her desires, she can live without him; the last words of the novel are "If he does not come, there will be life and love without him."

Mina is both a reflection and a reversal of Kilpatrick's *Child of the Night*. In both the vampire awakens unacknowledged sexual desires in a woman, but while Carol in Kilpatrick's novel finds herself by joining the vampire world, Mina finds herself in rejecting it. As evidenced by Karina, not all vampires are evil, but they are ensnared by the evil of Dracula and Illona, in which sexuality becomes predatory cruelty and self-indulgence. Mina comes to accept her sexuality as not simply normal but good—indeed, even to see it as holy, as her body and blood become one with the body and blood of Christ—she has no need for romantic love and domesticity. Unlike Carol, who wants community, Mina seeks freedom.

Mina is an "ultimate liberation" novel, as the end of sexual repression means the liberation of women and in fact humanity. Mina not only defeats Dracula but in doing so reclaims her own desire, body, and will. For Kilpatrick, Carol's encounter with Andre is an encounter with the "other" who also completes her; for Kiraly, the encounter with Dracula is an encounter with the self, which allows a reconciliation with masculinity as well as freedom. Dracula catalyzes Mina's sexual awakening, but he does so by corrupting sexuality into evil. By defeating him, Mina gains not only genuine freedom but, through accepting the goodness of herself, control over her future and the opportunity for meaningful ethical choice.

The liberation affirmed in *Mina* is not simply Mina's victory over Dracula but the liberation of our imaginations from the older forms of identity and value embodied in *Dracula*. While *Dracula* is indispensable to *Mina*, in the end there is no real chance of fidelity or even continuity. Dracula must die, and if *Dracula* lives, it is only because he is no longer what he was. Yet the past can only be made to yield up the future through accepting its power and using it to create our own stories.

"I'm not really good for anything"

While Newman and Simmons created counter-Dracula stories of the Count, Michael Almereyda's *Nadja* is a post-*Dracula* Dracula story, as the movie begins with his death and then follows the battle between his children, Nadja and Edgar, and the Van Helsing family. [3] When the movie begins, the Count is "alive" in New York, along with the two children by the one woman he ever loved. Nadja lives as a vampire, feeding and destroying even though she knows this existence is pointless, while Edgar has decided to abandon the vampire way, accepting that the choice may mean his death. In the first scene, Nadja picks up a man in a bar; they talk, she tells him of her pointless existence and her "bastard" of a father who still supports her. She recognizes that her life is trivial: "All these choices in our lives, everything is superficial," she says to the man moments before she kills him. At the same moment, Dr. Van Helsing, played by Peter Fonda as a drunken ex-hippie, kills Dracula; Nadja knows of this instantly through her telepathic contact with her father. Nadja and Renfield, her vampire companion, go to the morgue to claim Dracula's body though not, as Van Helsing fears, to revive him. Instead they burn the corpse so Nadja can finally be free of her father's influence, though she seems prepared to remain a vampire.

Van Helsing goes to his nephew, Jim, to get help in tracking down

120

Dracula's children. He tells him that while most of Dracula's children are monsters who fit right into contemporary society, because Nadja and Edgar are the product of genuine love they are more capable and dangerous than the others. Meanwhile, Nadja meets Jim's wife, Lucy, in a bar; they go back to Lucy and Jim's apartment where Nadja attacks/seduces her, making her a zombie slave. When Van Helsing and Jim realize what has happened, they follow Lucy to Edgar's apartment, where Nadja has gone to save her dying brother. Since Edgar now refuses to drink human blood, Nadja offers him the plasma Dracula developed from shark embryos to allow them to live without attacking humans—though she also seems to want to bring him back to life as a vampire. Edgar has fallen in love with Jim's sister Cassandra, who is working as his nurse, and he resists Nadja. After a battle in the apartment and a chase through the streets of Manhattan, Nadja and Renfield escape back to Transylvania with Cassandra as their prisoner; Lucy remains in her "brain fog" zombie state. Edgar agrees to help Van Helsing and Jim track down his sister, and they go to Transylvania. Van Helsing and Edgar stake Nadja while Jim battles Renfield, who is also finally impaled.

Unknown to everyone else, Nadja has literally transfused her identity into Cassandra ("the blood is the life" as in Stoker) and mysteriously lives on within her. The movie ends with a long shot of the humans standing on the steps of city hall after Edgar and Cassandra's marriage. We hear Nadja's voice-over, though the shot fades to a close-up of Cassandra's face, which dissolves into Nadja's face, then back into Cassandra's; we cannot tell who is really speaking. "I have walked beyond the sky. We are all animals but there is a better way to live. Sometimes at night I hear a voice in my head. Is it you Nadja? Is it true that the beyond, everything beyond is here in this life? I can't hear you. What's there? Is it only me? Is it myself?" Through Almereyda's transformation of Stoker's original, Dracula not only dies but becomes a dreamlike memory. While *Nadja* uses characters and situations from *Dracula* and loosely follows the plot, Alemereyda treats this material as if *Dracula* had never been written, as if his film is the "real" story of the Count; again, the palimpsest effect is a useful model. As does *Children of the Night*, *Nadja* reaffirms the humanity and spirituality concluding Stoker's novel and, at the same time, revises these nineteenth-century affirmations.

This sense of doubleness is expressed in the style of the movie. Visually *Nadja* alternates between realism and hallucination, echoing the poetic grotesqueness of *Eraserhead* and *The Elephant Man* (David Lynch was the executive producer), creating a dream world contiguous with but not exactly part of the ordinary world. Almereyda owes debts not just to Stoker and Lynch but to Andre Breton, from whose 1928 novel he takes both the title and the final lines of the movie. Shot in black and white, the action scenes are typically blurry and pixilated, a style that makes them appear surreal; other scenes are filmed in a sharply focused, realistic perspective. We are visually never in a single, unified world and are constantly reminded that the movie is both a vampire story and a poetic/critical reflection on that genre in the 1990s. *Nadja* defines the contemporary world itself as a pastiche, a kind of dream existence between life and death in which meaning and value have disappeared. While imprisoned in the castle in Transylvania, Cassandra reflects on the crisis of post-human existence. "The problem is we've lost our spirituality. We've lost contact with ourselves and what our purpose for existence is. We've lost contact with God and I don't mean God as an old man with a beard, a father and a punisher, but as a source, a spiritual stream of energy and light that links all things. We have a huge hole in ourselves. I don't know anyone who doesn't have a huge emptiness in their lives. We look away, otherwise you start asking yourself why does one day merge with another day? Why does a black night gather in the mouth? Why are all these people dead?"

Nadja merges the quest to kill the vampire with the vampire's own search for a better way to live; while Stoker and Coppola release Dracula into a spiritual realm, by killing Nadja Almereyda releases her into the chance for humanity, however ambiguous that may be. The movie is about the characters' search for humanity in the forms of self, love, and family, all of which have been lost in the contemporary world. Lucy's brother killed himself when he was twenty-one and her father abandoned her after being "born again." Van Helsing reveals he had an affair with his brother's wife and that Jim, who thinks he is Van Helsing's nephew, is really his son; Jim and Cassandra have lost touch with each other, as have Nadja and Edgar. Even Dracula lost his beloved in childbirth; after that, as Van Helsing says, "he didn't care about anything, it was just back to basics." The movie ends with an image of marriage and happy families, as the Van Helsings and the Draculas marry into each other's families (though Nadja and Cassandra have already been joined in a far more intimate way). The last image, a long shot, puts us at an extreme distance and angle to this family happiness.

Nadja almost becomes a slayer story, but the slayers ultimately fail to kill Nadja and don't even know they have failed. Nadja is both the enemy and ourselves, aware of the emptiness of her own existence and ending it through a form of suicide that leaves her disembodied awareness existing solely through another person. This is both the ultimate form of vampirism—the kind of possession that almost destroys Kiraly's Mina—and Nadja's return to humanity. The ambiguity of Cassandra's identity is the ambiguity of all identity. If there is no transcendental reality and we live in a merely human world, we must make its connections of love and family our reality. While on one hand *Nadja* affirms that we can be more than superficial, predatory animals, it also recognizes that even the "better way" of humanity does not bring us complete self-knowledge or the end of our uncertainty about who we really are. The secrecy of Nadja's escape into Cassandra and the resulting ambiguity mean, appropriately, Almereyda has chosen not to step out of the post-human situation but simply to affirm the "better way" within it. Similarly, *Dracula* fades into *Nadja,* and Stoker is there and not there at the same time.

Dracula Goes to College

Finally, we return to Stoker's novel, in a form encompassing what it was as well as what it may have to be to survive in the twenty-first century. In academia until quite recently, reading *Dracula* has been at best optional, for Stoker's novel has never had the canonical status of an *Emma* or *Portrait of a Lady.* With these works, you might watch the movie but you had to read the novel to get the "real" thing; with *Dracula,* any old movie would do. When I was in graduate school in 1972 at the University of Chicago, taking the final for a course in romantic poetry, the professor was reading *Dracula* while proctoring the exam. As I recall we thought this both goofy and exciting, for here was a cheap Dell paperback (with a startlingly blue-faced Count in profile on the cover) in the same room with Wordsworth and Coleridge. The fifty-cent paperback made clear that the novel had no real status; today, the hefty fourteen-dollar *Dracula: A Norton Critical Edition* is the first appearance of the novel in an edition that unquestionably confers academic respectability, affirming that Stoker's work is ready to join *Pride and Prejudice* and *David Copperfield* among the other Norton classics.[4]

It is useful to read the Norton *Dracula,* though literally faithful to Stoker, as a Dracula variation that lifts the novel from commercial pop-culture into the academic canon.[5] Norton's selection of the novel suggests its continuing imaginative presence in our culture, but more importantly, it affirms the power of critical analysis to create a progressive understanding of culture—in this case, through contemporary interpretations of a Victorian novel. The volume as a whole is a liberationist *Dracula,* though liberation comes from a critical understanding of *Dracula* rather than the embrace of the vampire. As the Norton edition makes clear, *Dracula* is our novel largely as a window on the past and our own cultural evolution, not as a contemporary story the way *Nadja* and *Mina* are.

In its elevation to literature, *Dracula* becomes an example of how the Victorians (and all generations) repress the truth, particularly the truths of sexuality and gender. The true story of *Dracula* is found in the critical essays, which reveal what the novel can only suggest in muffled and ambiguous ways. Victorian idealism and thrills are a ruse covering fears of evolutionary atavism, syphilis, and female sexuality, as well as an underlying homophobia and misogyny. Most importantly, the Victorian fears and anxieties are still ours, and by understanding this legacy we can continue in the process of putting those terrors to rest. The Norton's essays are in their own way as moralistic as Stoker, for the stripping away of illusions is the moral imperative of the academic enterprise, affirming that we have the power to make ourselves better people in a better world. As with the original it frames, the Norton *Dracula* is a fin de siècle book in its strong sense of transition and its need to view our own moment through the lens of the past. As with all the other Dracula variations in this chapter, the Norton *Dracula* uses Stoker's novel to provide historical perspective on the present as we turn toward the future.

The Norton *Dracula* is centered on current academic debates about sexual politics; aiding the progressive emancipation of sexuality from the Victorian insanity of repression is the purpose of this *Dracula.* The titles of the essays in the criticism section hint at how this *Dracula* reads: "Suddenly Sexual Women in Bram Stoker's *Dracula*" by Phyllis Roth; "'Kiss Me with

Those Red Lips': Gender and Inversion in Bram Stoker's *Dracula*" by Christopher Craft; "A Wilde Desire Took Me: The Homoerotic History of Dracula" by Talia Schaffer. A selection from Bram Dijkstra's *Idols of Perversity: Fantasies of Feminine Evil in Fin-de-Siècle Culture* also shows the Norton's stance. Stephen Arata's "The Occidental Tourist: *Dracula* and the Anxiety of Reverse Colonization" dovetails with the psychosexual cultural studies approach to the novel in dealing with another repressed fear exorcised by criticism. Thus *Dracula* becomes not only the revelation of the unVictorian Victorians, engulfed by a sexuality they could not represent directly or even acknowledge, but a step toward the liberation of sexuality, which has played such a large part in the transformations of twentieth-century culture. As "subversiveness" and "resistance" have become honorific in contemporary academia, the *Dracula* of the Norton edition becomes part, albeit largely unknowingly, of these activities.

I'm not saying that the edition is improperly biased in examining the novel in this way; issues of gender and sexuality are clearly part of the novel. Nor is it that these are bad articles or that their arguments are wrong. I am saying that this, like any attempt to make *Dracula* our story, is caught in a moment of self-revelation, in trying to find meaning in the present through an act of apparent fidelity to the past. When the Norton essays point out how Victorian ideology about biology, sexuality, men, women, gender, and love controlled what Stoker wrote, deforming the story from our point of view, they tame it by accounting for its remoteness from us under the rubrics of repression and progress.

Stoker's ideas and attitudes are Victorian—but in the same incoherent way our ideas and attitudes are late twentieth century. An analysis that looks at *Dracula* in terms of crisis, avoidance, and repression implies a progressive teleology that sees Stoker's novel as a tentative step toward the late twentieth century. Reading *Dracula* in this way, as our novel, allows us to understand what changes and transformations the surface of our culture hides. We are still Victorians with everything to learn about ourselves. Indeed, the many vampire stories that in the end affirm Stoker's values of family, spirituality, and love suggest there is truth to this assessment, though the meaning of these terms has changed substantially in contemporary versions. The Norton's editors and essayists hope, in a modest way, to use *Dracula* to help create new a culture that paradoxically, might not need

Dracula to reveal its desires, even while implicitly accepting that the irrational, inarticulate, fantastical story is more attractive to us than the rational understanding gleaned from it.

From the Norton point of view, *Dracula* endures because it remains endlessly tantalizing. Though charged with meaning, it will never on its own say directly what we need to read. *Dracula* has become bizarre to us, needing interpretation because in its Victorian strangeness it affirms that Good shall triumph over Evil, that self-control and spiritual community protect us, and that nobody in their right mind would want to be a vampire. And yet we still need *Dracula.* In demystifying Stoker's novel, the Norton embrace of *Dracula* defines the uneasy relation between our hopes for progress, liberation, and rationality and our need for tradition, continuity, and imagination.

Dracula Begins His Second Century

Dracula's continuing status as a symbolic presence is made clear in the recent Dracula variations *Shadow of the Vampire* and *Dracula 2000,* two movies that frame the vampire story as a reflection on the history of the twentieth century and on the Dracula story as a part of that history. In these two movies Dracula serves as the symbol for both the ancient past that soulless modernity kills and absorbs and the buried secret of modernity itself, its despair that its sins can be forgiven. The premise of *Shadow of the Vampire* is that Murnau found a real vampire to play the Orlock/Dracula role in *Nosferatu.* Willem Dafoe's Max Schreck is a nasty hobgoblin, the image of the fantastical past, while John Malkovich's Murnau is the scientist who seeks to place "all our memories on film." Though Schreck slaughters the cast and crew as filming progresses, it becomes clear that Murnau, the technician-scientist dressed in a white lab coat, is far more monstrous than the ugly little bundle of desires embodied by the vampire. Modernity, in all its decadence and technology, finally devours the vampire, loses its soul, and, through film, enshrines the loss by immortalizing and transforming the image of the monster. That image represents the twentieth century's loss of its soul to a bloodless, mechanical modernity.

In *Dracula 2000,* Van Helsing has guarded the coffin of the unkillable Dracula since the nineteenth century, staying alive through injections of vampire blood, and now he must pass the guardianship on to his daughter, Mary. Dracula escapes his vault during an attempted robbery of Van Helsing's business (appropriately, antiques). Because Mary has vampire blood in her veins, she is the object of Dracula's desire and also a potential bride for him. This Dracula is fashionably erotic, a monstrous seducer who, though chained in his coffin, embodies the true spirit of modernity: all style, no substance, mere predation for predation's sake. In the end Mary conquers Dracula by discovering his secret: he is Judas Iscariot, condemned to eternal life not because he betrayed Christ but because he despaired that Christ's mercy could extend even to him. There is no reason to think we are meant to take this return to Christianity terribly seriously, but it does capture a generalized sense that the twentieth century is marked by the failure of spiritual values ("God is dead") and that the time has come to put away such despair.

Dracula remains the image of the strange, the dangerous, the mysterious, but he is increasingly present only in spirit. The real world presses in upon him, whether in the form of social change, technology, pathology, feminism, or critical analysis. Though the outlines remain, they are drastically altered. Indeed, a cynic might see *Dracula*'s canonization as literature as the final stake. But it would be rash and pointless speculation to conclude that *Dracula* and Dracula are about to become museum pieces rather than persisting as dynamic parts of our culture. There is no reason to assume that academia's uses of the novel will continue in the directions sketched out in the Norton *Dracula*. It is true that the novel's idiom, both literary and cultural, is becoming more and more remote from us; the novel is no longer even the literature of the previous century, after all. In addition to new vampires and new Draculas, we have created new stories of the slayer, whose language is closer to ours. But as Count Dracula has yet to stay buried, any report of his death would be, as always, mere rumor.

6

RETURN OF THE SLAYER

During the ascendance of the vampire as protagonist, slayers began getting some distinctly bad press; Stoker's heroes and their descendants were, by the 1960s, being transformed into antiques, exemplars of Victorian repression and sentimentality even in the Hammer movies. Slayers became the gang of hysterical idiots in *The Dracula Tape*, the brutal gardener in *Blood for Dracula*, the ridiculous Dr. Jeffrey Rosenberg of *Love at First Bite*, the mad Uncle Cuda of *Martin*, or the tragically ineffective Sarah Roberts of *The Hunger* and Jonathan Harker of the 1979 *Nosferatu*. Slayers simply disappeared from some works as the vampire's story became our story. But however much distance we have put between Stoker's repressed Christians and ourselves, the slayer returns when the vampire again becomes something we can call Evil, the terror of the post-human future, the face of a world dominated by violent, feral intellect.

The return of the slayer is part of the continuing, convoluted search for heroic figures that has preoccupied American culture for the last thirty years; this upsurge in interest in the slayer at the end of the century parallels the popularity of the heroic films of Tom Hanks and Kevin Costner. Since the slayer is locked in struggle with the vampire and the vampire had to be transformed in order to flourish in the late twentieth century, so did the vampire slayer. Since vampires had a double existence as protagonists and monsters, slayers also became self-divided figures, struggling as much with their own nature as with the vampire; indeed, some vampire slayers such as Nick Knight and Sonja Blue are also vampires. The vampire slayer is not just a hero but an exploration of the troubled state of heroism in contemporary America, where the celebrity has crowded the traditional hero from our view.

It's easy to be a vampire, particularly a post-human one; as La Croix tells Nick Knight in *Forever Knight,* you simply "give in to the animal in your blood," or as Mae tells Caleb in *Near Dark,* "don't think about it, just let your instincts take over." It is hard to be a slayer, though; today, slayers typically begin the battle with the undead as lost or damaged people without any sustaining beliefs or values. As they live in a blighted post-human world where tradition and progress have already failed, the slayers' only source of meaning and order is the late twentieth century's last great explanatory narrative, the conspiracy story. Giving in and not thinking about it is exactly what a slayer cannot do. To be a slayer means accepting one's own mortality; in the end one fights the vampire for the right not only to live as a human but to die a natural death.

Contemporary slayer stories are about the search for a model of humanity that allows us to reach beyond compulsion and exercise meaningful ethical choice, including the decision to affirm life while accepting death. Religion rarely provides the basis for such an ideal; today's slayers are hardly ever Christians. Even if they wave the cross at the vampires, their spiritual qualities, if any, are typically represented by imaginary, syncretic mythologies that only have a literary existence. For the slayer, the source of human values is the web of relationships in which we live; whether defined as friendship, family, or community, this web of relationships is so valuable that the slayer will not merely kill for it but die for it. If sexuality represented humans' paradigmatic ethical choice for Stoker's vampire hunters, the ethical issue for the contemporary slayer is violence. The post-human vampire is addicted to violence—not sex—and the slayer must retaliate with violence against violence, the stake against the fangs. In this, they again become the vampire's double and risk becoming as addicted to the power and pleasure of violence as their opponent. Yet the slayers' ability to refrain from violence and their willingness to die for their own humanity, the two things the vampire cannot do, distinguish the slayers' violence from the vampires'.

Trauma and loss, central motifs in American culture over the last three decades, are the emotional keynotes of contemporary slayers, damaged people for whom morality and heroism come at a high cost and yield, at best, uncertain rewards. The special quality of the slayer's trauma lies in the double horror of losing family, friends, and loved ones and also discovering that humans are vampires' prey, a realization that transforms the slayer's whole world. In *Dracula,* the creation of the band of slayers and the defeat of the Count heal the trauma of Lucy's death and subsequent staking as a vampire. Mina's vampire infection is cleansed and the peaceful order of England restored. Though Quincey Morris dies, his sacrifice is memorialized and honored in the naming of Mina and Jonathan Harker's child, the sign of hope in the future. The contemporary slayer's trauma, however, rarely heals. Caleb in *Near Dark* and, to lesser extents, Sonja in *Midnight Blue* and Ben Mears in *'Salem's Lot* are exceptions to this trend. Virtually all contemporary slayers work in secret; there are no public rewards for slaying, and they can never be truly integrated into ordinary life again—particularly those slayers who are also vampires. For many, vampire slaying becomes their ordinary life.

Mina Harker and Abraham Van Helsing are the ancestors of today's slayers, but because our ideas about gender have changed, their descendants have changed. We have seen a number of versions of Mina: she has become Dracula's lover; a doctor and mother; a liberated woman whose blood, sexual and holy, can kill the vampire. None of these characters, though, is really a slayer, even the ones who kill Dracula; Coppola's Mina releases Dracula rather than kills him, and Kiraly's Mina lets Dracula's own need destroy him. Contemporary slayers Buffy Summers and Sonja Blue are direct descendants of Mina Harker, but they are also cousins to Lt. Ellen Ripley of the *Alien* movie series, popular culture's undisputed champion female defender of humanity and monster-whacker. Ripley has emerged as a fusion of the heroic warrior with post-feminist ideas about who and what women are. As in the *Alien* movies, female slayers' stories aren't about women acting like men but about redefining the hero; the slayer wrestles with the meaning of femininity, particularly the relation between femininity and violence.[1]

If Ripley is the contemporary inspiration for the female slayer, male slayers are descended not only from Van Helsing, that eccentric outsider, but also from Mel Gibson's Road Warrior. The Road Warrior, cast adrift in a blighted world, unappreciated and unloved, saving the human commu-

nity but never a part of it, defines the deeply distressed situation of traditional warrior masculinity in a culture that has less and less place for that
particular heroic quality. If feminism outlines the female slayer, the male
vampire slayer is silhouetted against the background of the Vietnam War;
both Carl Kolchak of *The Night Stalker* and Ben Mears of *'Salem's Lot* are
imagined from an antiwar position, while Jack Crow and the members of
Team Crow in *Vampire$* draw on the conventions of the traumatized vet,
which have such currency in American culture. Both versions of the slayer
struggle to find an identity and a place in a world that seems more and
more the home of the undead rather than the brave.

"This nut *thinks* he's a vampire!"

The first truly contemporary slayer appears in the first unmistakable intersection of the vampire slayer story with the conspiracy narrative. Perhaps
unsurprisingly, it appeared in the same medium as *Dark Shadows* and was
the work of the same producer. On January 11, 1972, *The Night Stalker*, a
Dan Curtis production based on a then-unpublished novel by Jeff Rice
and a screenplay by Richard Matheson, aired on ABC and became the
highest rated made-for-television movie up to that time. [2] *The Night Stalker*,
unlike *Dark Shadows,* is overtly political, making the vampire story into a
tale of government power and deception.

The Night Stalker is a remarkable piece of storytelling, elegant, collo-
quial, and direct, narrated by reporter Carl Kolchack in a voice-over. In
contemporary Las Vegas, Kolchack begins pursuing the story of a series of
young women who have been kidnapped from the Strip and found drained
of their blood. Unruly, anarchic, and probably alcoholic, Kolchack is initially interested in a big murder story to end the downward spiral of his
career and get him back on a New York City paper. At first he concludes
these strange murders are the work of a madman who thinks he's a vampire, then Kolchak realizes that the suspect, Janos Skorzeny, actually is a
vampire. Throughout the movie, Kolchack fights the city officials who want
to keep the murders quiet and certainly don't want any talk of vampires to
alarm the tourists, who are the lifeblood of the city. Kolchak stalks Skorzeny
to his lair, stakes him, and writes the most sensational news story in history—only to have the government suppress it, make his girlfriend disap-

pear, and run him out of town by threatening to prosecute him for the "murder" of a man who was only wanted for questioning.

Darren McGaven plays an energetic, over-the-top Kolchack who wears a seersucker suit with a battered straw hat and tennis shoes; he even makes up an anti-vampire kit of stakes, holy water, and crosses for the police chief and sheriff. Kolchak is an outsider with no respect for authority, a loner who sees how things really are. If Barnabas Collins is the reluctant vampire, Kolchak is the involuntary Van Helsing. He has much of Van Helsing's eccentricity but is young enough to also have a beautiful girlfriend who thinks to get vampire books from the library—though he does the vampire hunting on his own. While *The Night Stalker* doesn't directly address the issue of masculinity (in 1971 it wasn't clear that such an issue existed), Kolchak is clearly an unconventional hero whose eccentricity was striking to an early-seventies audience.

Though Skorzeny is a European vampire, complete with cape, this is

Darren McGavin as the anxious vampire hunter Carl Kolchak in *The Night Stalker* (1972).

a primal American story since Kolchak's vampire hunt begins as a search for the big score. The portrayal of Las Vegas and the vampire, low tech and low budget by contemporary standards, is the visual equivalent of idiomatic American English. The movie's impact is based in its fusion of the vampire story with Las Vegas, which, as Hunter Thompson claimed in 1971, was at the heart of the American Dream. Las Vegas is devoted to responding to all forms of desire; the Strip is a world of permanent vacation where everything is for sale or involves gambling; both the vampire and the town leave people drained. The Las Vegas Strip is designed to look good at night, but in the daytime it seems empty and flat; it is the perfect city for the vampire. Skorzeny is at home in this iconic American fantasy city, the creation of the mob, the home of the Rat Pack, the hipster's swinging town.

Though Skorzeny attacks young women, we have no sense of him as a sexual predator, let alone a romantic figure; his victims are merely food, no different than the bottles of plasma he steals from the hospital. One victim is actually hooked up to an IV, fulfilling Dracula's vision of Mina as a "bountiful wine press." Skorzeny, who never speaks but hisses when confronted, is an animalistic and purely evil; and in spite of his supernatural qualities, he is obviously not that hard to defeat, as he is staked by a terrified, out-of-shape reporter.

Skorzeny is an early post-human vampire who highlights and makes manifest the evils of the society he preys upon. His existence is not in opposition to the human world but actually abetted by it, for he is simply an embodiment of it. The terror and paranoia that usually surround the vampire are transferred to figures of authority, for whom the vampire becomes, finally, the metaphor. Las Vegas, the all-night town, serves up prey with striking regularity, and its official, institutional culture effectively helps Skorzeny hide. Scarier than the vampire roaming the night is the fact that the establishment is in charge, the newspapers are the city officials' lackeys, and the public is never going to get the truth about anything, even if the information might save lives. Two years later, *Jaws* tells a similar story, but *The Night Stalker* is far more skeptical and ominous because the cover-up is never exposed, and the hero, though he survives, is defeated in his fight against the real enemy, the Las Vegas elite.

The establishment acts in ways strikingly similar to the vampire. The official version of events makes Kolchack, not Skorzeny, a murderer, and when the government makes his girlfriend disappear, it eerily recalls how Skorzeny made young women vanish from the Strip. The government keeps secrets, makes people disappear, and is finally undefeatable. From Watergate emerged *All the President's Men,* the heroic narrative of reporters who triumph over the power of the secret cabal and get their story printed. But it has been *The Night Stalker* and its descendants, including perhaps *JFK,* that have provided the more enduring narrative of our society's power structure.

While in *Dracula* the vampire brought the characters to their truest, best selves, *The Night Stalker* reverses this pattern (except in the case of Kolchak). Rather than a community of heroes pooling their knowledge toward common cause, *The Night Stalker* portrays a cabal of powerful government and commercial interests keeping secrets for their own profit and authority. One of the central events in *Dracula* is Mina's collating of all the characters' narratives so they can understand what is going on, but the creation of a shared narrative is thwarted in *The Night Stalker.* The press conferences in which Kolchak confronts the authorities are exercises in disinformation, and when Kolchak has proof of the vampire's existence, the true story is suppressed.

Kolchak's courage in facing the vampire and discovering the truth is erased as if it never happened; Kolchak is almost as defeated as Skorzeny. He has no friends, no lover, and no future; this slayer's only reward is that he knows the truth. Las Vegas will go on as before, but Kolchack is excluded from the city of the American Dream, the big score. If *The Night Stalker* resembles any other vampire story it is *Blood for Dracula,* for like Morrissey's movie, *The Night Stalker* renders its heroic tale in elegiac terms; there is no community left for the hero to defend, no one to sacrifice for, not even a real recognition of what he has done, except his editor's awkward acknowledgment that Kolchak is a great reporter. All Kolchak has left is the truth that he can never tell. Kolchak has risen to the occasion, but he can't get anyone else to even admit the occasion existed. After this, all Kolchak can do is tell his vampire story like some ancient mariner in a straw hat. In the final scene we see a weary Kolchak in his motel room concluding recording his story on cassettes. This is simply a great final shot, Kolchak tossing the last tape on the table, telling us to believe it or not.

"The town knew darkness"

Stephen King's *'Salem's Lot*[3] was a follow-up to the best-selling *Carrie*. In his second novel, King went back to a classic of horror, both for commercial reasons and to define his relation to the tradition of horror writing. From one point of view, *'Salem's Lot* is a straightforward vampire thriller whose descent from Dracula is directly acknowledged. The vampire Barlow and his human servant, Straker, come to 'Salem's Lot planning to take over and make its inhabitants into their vampire servants; Ben Mears and other residents have to stop them. Yet the fact that *'Salem's Lot* was begun in October 1972 and finished in June of 1975, bracketed by the ends of the Vietnam War and Watergate, suggests there is more to the story; the state of America was on King's mind as he wrote. This is also a regionalist novel in which King begins dealing with his relation to Maine and his childhood there. As the central character is a novelist, King examines the nature of fiction and the value of horror stories—particularly vampire stories—in the early 1970s. *'Salem's Lot* is a novel about what vampires and vampire slayers meant in contemporary American culture, why vampires once again appealed to us during its time.

As with *The Night Stalker*, *'Salem's Lot* resonates against the iconography of an archetypal American place. The town's two names, Jerusalem's Lot and its diminutive, 'Salem's Lot, recall colonial New England as both the City on the Hill and the scene of witch trial hysteria (the town is actually named for a pig who liked to root around on the spot where it was built). Through this synecdoche of New England history, King invites us to see America through the lens of the vampire story. The vampire, though once again European, only brings out what is already present in the town, what is already in America. And as with *The Night Stalker*, the community the slayers defend has withered away long before the battle against the vampires begins.

Ben Mears, the slayer, is still suffering from the death of his wife in an auto accident for which he blames himself. Having lost his inspiration, the novelist has come back to 'Salem's Lot to write about a still-troubling childhood experience, a ghostly vision of death in the reputedly haunted Marston House (previously owned by Hubie Marston, devil-worshipping gangster), in the hopes of restarting his imagination and dealing with his grief. The novel is also, then, about Ben's attempts to find himself as a writer by re-

turning to his past. Dealing with fear, guilt, childhood, and artistic voca-
tion, Ben's return to 'Salem's Lot is a search for himself, his artistic voice,
his past, and the ability to love. Ben's situation is, in King's phrase, the
plight of "the artistic male" in a culture of hypermasculinity in which "queer"
is the most damning epithet imaginable.

The theme of masculine identity is also part of the insistent allusions
to the Vietnam War; King, who was active in antiwar protests at the University of Maine, likely assumed that such references would ring with im-
mediacy for his readers. The narrator makes ten references to the war, which,
though it was largely out of sight for the townspeople (except for the one or
two boys who didn't come back), is clearly the cultural context in which
King imagines the vampire invasion of small town America. Implicitly,
Ben, the artistic male who didn't go to war, is contrasted not only with the
other men in the town but also with the young men who did go to Vietnam, particularly those who didn't come back. The novel's overt concern
with the artist contrasting with its shadowy figure of the soldier, who lingers on the margin of the story, reflects that generation's defining of masculinity and heroism under the criteria of who went to Vietnam and who
didn't.

'Salem's Lot also contrasts the understanding of evil as it appears in
realism and in fantasy. In a section entitled "The Town Knew Darkness,"
King enumerates all the evil, corruption, and secrets of the town; much of
the first half of the novel is saturated with the alcoholism, child abuse,
wife-beating, homophobia, petty bullying, and dishonesty that characterizes the Lot. The ideal of "small town America" is a threadbare illusion,
and realistic sections of the novel are grim and depressing; King reveals the
horrors of small town life with the energy of an angry native son. When
Father Callaghan, the alcoholic priest, meditates on the relation between
the ordinary day-to-day evils of the town and the possibility of a giant
conspiracy he might combat, he defines his frustration with reality as well
as the general frustration of realism.

He had been pining for a Challenge. The new priests had theirs: racial discrimination, women's liberation, even gay liberation; poverty,
insanity, illegality. They made him uncomfortable. The only socially
conscious priests he felt at ease with were the ones who had been

militantly opposed to the war in Viet Nam. Now that their cause had become obsolete, they sat around and discussed marches and rallies the way old married couples discuss their honeymoon or the first train ride. But Callaghan was neither a new priest nor an old one; he found himself cast in the role of a traditionalist who can no longer trust his own basic principles. He wanted to lead a division in the army of—who? God, right, goodness, they were names for the same thing—into battle against EVIL. He wanted issues and battle lines and never mind standing in the cold outside supermarkets to hand out leaflets about the lettuce boycott or the grape strike. He wanted to see EVIL, with its cerements of deception cast aside, with every feature of its visage clear. He wanted to slug it out toe to toe with EVIL. . . .

But there were no battles. There were only skirmishes of vague resolution. And EVIL did not wear one face but many, and all of them were vacuous and more often than not the chin was slicked with drool. . . .

The great social, moral, and spiritual battles of the age boiled down to Sandy McDougall slamming her snot-nosed kid in the corner and the kid would grow up and slam his own kid in the corner, world without end, hallelujah, chunky peanut butter. Hail Mary, full of grace, help me win this stock car race.

Callaghan's drunken monologue, trailing off into mumbles of popular culture, defines the hopelessness that results when tradition and future collapse, the fabric of community has unraveled, and the world becomes a place of endless horrors that are roughly identical with ignorance, poverty, and general human meanness. Just as Callaghan is frustrated with reality, we become frustrated with the novel's realism: these are facts, and there seems to be nothing we can do about then. King offers us the regional realism not just to make us want a vampire tale but to show us why we want it. When the story turns away from Ben Mear's emotional life and the town's sociology to the battle with bloodsucking monsters, our pleasure increases dramatically.

When Father Callaghan confronts Barlow, he finally collapses before

EVIL, but Ben Mears is more successful. He finally goes into the old Marston House in search of Susan Norton, his new girlfriend; and while he can't save her, he does save a young boy, Mark Petrie, who has followed Susan there in hopes of avenging his family, who Barlow has murdered. Mark is a profile of Ben as a boy: intelligent, reserved, artistic, fascinated with horror (he has a collection of Aurora Monster models, including Dracula). His first appearance in the novel is on the school playground when he defeats the school bully who calls him "four-eyed queer-boy." When Ben and Mark face Barlow in the depths of the Marston House, Ben is possessed by the primal life force, the "White Light." "A hard sense of sureness clasped him, a feeling of inevitable rightness, of *whiteness.* For the first time in weeks he felt he was no longer groping through fogs of belief and unbelief, sparring with a partner whose body was too insubstantial to sustain blows." Ben the artistic male becomes the warrior, powerful and righteous. Under the influence of the force, he hacks open the door to Eva Miller's root cellar, where he confronts Barlow; before they attack Barlow, Ben tells Mark that he loves him.

A homoerotic reading of this moment is easy, but King takes the story in another direction; Mears's love for Mark is not sexual but parental, extending to the boy as affection that allows Mears to love himself in filling the role of Mark's murdered father. (Ben's father died when he was young, so each is searching for reconciliation between father and son.) Throughout the novel King makes clear that homophobia is pervasive in the town; his concern is to affirm that not all close and loving relations between men are homosexual in nature. Insisting on the homoerotic content of Ben and Mark's relationship would simply invert the town's pervasive homophobia by assuming that any man who cares for another must be "queer"—whether that is defined as positive or negative. King is extraordinarily clumsy in side-stepping this assumption, because at the moment when Ben extends his love to Mark and himself, it becomes clear that Susan, who is the most poorly written character in the novel, has existed only to establish that Ben is heterosexual; once that function is performed, she has to be killed off, as King apparently can't figure out how to include her in the relationship between Ben and Mark. [4]

In the end, Ben and Mark escape 'Salem's Lot but return to burn the town down and destroy the rest of the vampires. They do so realizing that there is no assurance this will end their struggle, but that if they don't, the vampires will certainly continue to multiply and kill. The conclusion offers the satisfaction of both heroic action and ethical purpose, the creation of a new family in which father and son are reconciled, and the awareness that the struggle against evil is endless. It is not difficult to see in this slayer story the fantasy of moral and ethical ideals that lost their basis in reality during the war and Watergate, as well as the aspiration to a new sense of manhood apart from the figure of the soldier.

Ben is better off than Carl Kolchak; in gaining a son and getting his novel (presumably *'Salem's Lot*) published, he has a greater share in the future. But both *The Night Stalker* and *'Salem's Lot* emerge from disillusionment with and distrust of the Vietnam War, the failure—whichever side you were on—of the indisputable reality of American power and goodness. That reality is now the object of fantasy and can be reclaimed only in the imagination. For King, a realistic novel about 'Salem's Lot and about America would be a tale of hopelessness; only the arrival of the vampires makes it possible to localize evil so it can be fought, makes it possible for Ben resolve his fears and anxieties by becoming a slayer. Both *The Night Stalker* and *'Salem's Lot* acknowledge that in reality there are no vampires or slayers, but this reality has no answers for us. Unlike Father Callaghan's alcohol-fueled nostalgia, the slayer story becomes meaningful by affirming the community, the hero, and ethical values while self-reflexively recognizing their passing from the real world into fantasy.

"Don't think about it, just let your instincts take over."

Kathryn Bigelow's first film, *Near Dark* (1987),[5] is one of the few slayer stories in which the triumph of Good seems unequivocal. Superbly written and shot, on its simplest level *Near Dark* is a cautionary story about a young man tempted to go bad because of his attraction to a young woman who has fallen in with "bad companions," i.e. vampires. *Near Dark* bears a family resemblance to *Fright Night* as a young man's initiation tale, but its focus shifts from adolescent sexuality and the perils of adulthood to the nature of violence and contemporary American identity, placing it in line with *The Night Stalker* and *'Salem's Lot*. *Near Dark* is also one of the earliest slayer stories in which the slayer is also, at least temporily, a vampire; unlike

Charley Brewster in *Fright Night,* Caleb has the chance to be immortal if he will forgo his soul.

Caleb meets Mae one night outside a bar; enchanted and infatuated, he takes her to see his horse, which is instinctively frightened of her. When Mae suddenly bites Caleb, he turns vampire immediately in a violent seizure. He tries to get home; in a terrifying scene he crosses the fields of the farm in early daylight, his flesh beginning to smolder. Before he makes it, though, the vampires track him down and take him on board their RV. At first they intend to kill him, but Mae shows them that she has turned him; as Caleb is one of them, the vampires let him live. Though Mae feeds him with her own blood in two erotic scenes, the vampires make clear that what they do is kill, and if Caleb won't follow suit, they will toss him out in the daylight to burn to death. Mae comforts Caleb by telling him that all killing means is letting instinct take over. Caleb hates the idea of killing and wants to return to his family, but as his feelings for Mae increase and he realizes he is no longer human, he cannot break away. After Caleb's family finds him and his humanity is restored by his father, Loy, the vampires kidnap his sister Sarah in revenge. Caleb tracks them down, and Mae, realizing she loves Caleb, turns against her vampire family and rescues Sarah. Caleb kills the rest of the vampires in a pitched battle, and Mae also returns to her human state.

Like *The Night Stalker* and *'Salem's Lot,* this is an assertively American vampire story, but *Near Dark* removes any hint of Dracula or European vampire influence. The world of the movie is completely secular and contemporary, with vampirism the result of a blood infection rather than a supernatural transformation. While *'Salem's Lot* and *The Night Stalker* use archetypal American towns as their symbol of American culture, *Near Dark* fuses the vampire story with a displaced myth, the Western, each revising the other. [6] After Peckinpaugh's *The Wild Bunch* and Leone's series of "spaghetti westerns," the western became an anachronism in American culture for almost two decades, except for Clint Eastwood's continued work in the genre. *Unforgiven* marked its return to prominence, though not as the central American genre anymore. If *Near Dark* recalls any particular Western, it's *The Searchers,* which is also a story of the hunt for a young person torn between two worlds, two identities, two versions of America and its past.

The stark beauty of the movie's visual world is matched by the directness and tautness of a story about people who live near the dividing line between human and post-human. In *Near Dark,* the West, like Las Vegas and 'Salem's Lot, positions the vampire in relation to a powerfully resonant American place. This is a world of big skies and vast plains, a spare natural space of which humans have only a small share; the sense of landscape's meaning is another link to the westerns, particulary John Ford's. This is the modern West of motels and bars with neon signs as well as the natural West, but it is also self-consciously the West as an American symbol, the place where Americans go to find themselves imaginatively. *Near Dark* takes place mostly at night and during the twilight hours, presenting a world of moonlight and lightning, neon and headlights, a plane of vision bisected by a flat horizon. From the cold blue of night and the bloodred of sunrise and sunset, the tableau shifts to a warm golden dawn after the vampires have been vanquished.

Just as the movie uses two genres to mirror each other, the vampires and the humans are also mirror images. The vampires are a roaming bandit gang, a strange and scary family that recalls Peckinpaugh's "wild bunch." Though Mae has been added to the gang only four years earlier, the vampires are essentially nineteenth-century people, the original settlers of the Old West. Jessie, the leader, was a Civil War solider and Severn was, or pretends to have been, a gunfighter before he was turned into a vampire as a young man. Jessie's companion, a woman called Diamondback, and Homer, who is stuck in early adolescence, seem to have been together for a long time. But with their RV and motel-to-motel lifestyle, they are also the modern descendants of the West gone bad, post-human Americans living a rootless and pointless existence without meaningful connection to their environment, intelligent animals running on instinct and bloodlust, traveling in search of "fun." These vampires look easy to reject: filthy and indifferent to their surroundings, they have no ambitions comparable to Dracula's Kingdom of the Undead, nor any of the style or glamour associated with Lestat, who in 1987 was at the height of his celebrity. Their posthumanity as vampires has neither ennobled them nor made them sophisticated or self-aware; they are ordinary people given over to a completely predatory existence.

At the same time, these post-human vampires look distressingly fa-

miliar and have recognizable human qualities. While they recall the canni-
bal families of Tobe Hooper's *Texas Chainsaw Massacre* and Wes Craven's
The Hills Have Eyes, they bear a distant relation to the more romantic Bar-
row gang of *Bonnie and Clyde.* They interact with each other as a human
family would; the nightmare family is still a family. Jessie and Severn, always sarcastically calling each other "son" and "grandpa," are locked in an
unresolvable Oedipal conflict sprawling across the decades. Diamondback
has a strange, out-of-place maternal feeling for Homer, who has not been a
child for years, possibly centuries. Diamondback and Jessie are like an old
married couple; at the end, as they burn together, she takes his hand and
whispers, in a moment both pathetic and grotesque, "good times" before
they explode in a cascade of orange fire.

The monstrous but recognizable family is contrasted with Caleb's.
Loy is a loving, if strict, father, a farmer and veterinarian; Sarah, a spunky
kid who adores Caleb as he adores her. When the two families cross paths
in a motel (Loy and Sarah, in unconscious imitation of the vampires, roam
Oklahoma in their truck looking for Caleb and his mysterious kidnap-
pers), Caleb chooses his real family and, through Loy's homespun scientific
process of combining massive blood transfusions with love, is brought back
across and made human again. While the vampires are the family we fear,
Caleb, Loy, and Sarah are the family we idealize. Yet this makes them more
remote from us than the vampires, for we recognize that they are what we
imagine the legacy of the Old West to be. While they are modern—Loy
uses science, albeit improvised, to save Caleb—they are also pure nostalgic
fantasy. We see much less of them than the vampires because the dream of
the ideal family can withstand less examination than the nightmare of the
horrific one.

The movie's central moment occurs when the vampires torture and
kill a group of humans in roadside bar. The scene is extraordinarily brutal:
when the waitress asks Jessie if he wants another drink he says yes, laughing
as he slices her throat and holding her head as she bleeds into his beer glass.
We're made to feel the fear and suffering with the humans, and the vampires, smeared with blood and leering, are far from gorgeous fiends. After
the other vampires have butchered the rest of the people in the bar, Mae
turns to a terrified young cowboy who has been rooted to his spot behind
the pool table throughout the whole scene. She dances with him, treats

him gently, and then, having made Caleb feel jealous, offers him the cow-boy for his first feeding.

During the initial moments of terrorizing the bar, Caleb is ill at ease and wants only to leave; like us he suspects, though he does not really know, what is coming. Caleb takes no part in the massacre, and though his jealousy makes him approach the cowboy, when he looks into the young man's frightened face he sees what none of the vampires can—an image of himself—and he cannot kill; this moment of awareness is striking, particulary in the midst of the intoxicating spectacle of violence. The scene casts Caleb as a version of the western hero who conquers his violent in-stincts, as Ethan Edwards finally does at the end of *The Searchers.* Through the spectacle of violence Bigelow also creates the ethical effect of the movie; we not only recognize Caleb's decision intellectually but, drawn into the chaotic emotions and sensations constituting that moment, we feel its meaning.

Near Dark affirms the love of the family and the power of that love over the destructive power of predation. The good family triumphs over the grotesque one, the ideal Americans over the degenerate ones, the best version of the West triumphs over the worst. One could argue that the western ultimately triumphs over the vampire story, with the slayer inte-grated into the figure of the cowboy and homesteader, making *Near Dark* a "Republican" slayer story. [7] Indeed, in 1987 *Near Dark* may have seemed a naive appeal to search for traditional values. On the other hand, though the film was highly praised, its mediocre reception at the box office, partly due to its limited distribution and the lack of big name stars, can be attrib-uted to the fact that the movie is too disturbing to be successful solely as a "family values" movie.

The vampires are uncomfortably close to being the film's real repre-sentations of Americans. By the end of the movie we understand that as horrible as they are, they are also us. In its images of vampires burning in the light of day and Mae's restoration at dawn, the movie affirms what we want to be truth—not reality. The movie does examine what it means to be human: Caleb's choice to reject instinct and his and Mae's escape from the vampires aren't undercut; the movie embraces the values of love, empathy, and family. But it also sets before us our competing fantasies of who we are, using the figures of the cowboy and vampire. Both the human and the vampire families come from the same primal American source, emerging directly out of the American past and its traditions. It's no less American to be a vampire than to be a cowboy.

"I know there's a God. I just don't understand him."

John Steakley's novel *Vampire$* [8] struggles to return the slayer story to a Christian framework, but the novel is at war with itself, for Steakley's real sense of value lies in the heroic warrior ideal, in which combat is the highest expression of masculinity. Steakley's vampire hunters, called "Team Crow" after their leader, are among the clearest examples of the slayer as an idealized version of the Vietnam vet. These are vampire slayers who fight on, unacknowledged, in a war no one wants to admit is happening. Unlike Kolchak and Mears, who are forced to become slayers by circumstances, Steakley's slayers are heroes by nature who have sought out slaying as a deadly calling, even though they realize there is no way they can survive the repeated encounters with vampires. The novel charts the gradual decimation of the team, beginning with a horrendous massacre after an apparently successful vampire hunt. The slayer's acceptance of mortality and the need for self-sacrifice have their most extreme expression here, partly because of this idealization of the warrior and partly because the novel is caught in a nostalgic anger about the loss of traditional ideals. Jack Crow's frustration with God still lingers at the end of *Vampire$,* passed on to the new team leader, William Charles Felix.

Team Crow works secretly with the Catholic Church. These stake-wielding Jesuits directly serve the Pope, who they call The Man. Steakley defines the conflict between the humans and vampires in theological terms as a war between Good and Evil, the Catholic Church against the Devil; though when dramatized, this opposition takes on a sociological quality, the traditional versus the contemporary. A former CIA/DEA/NSA agent, Jack Crow's extraordinary bravery makes him the greatest vampire slayer, but as the novel opens, the vampires have figured out who Crow is and have decided not simply to kill him but to bring him over and make him a master vampire. Vampires aren't Team Crow's only opponents, though; despite the fact that the small towns of North America are infested with nests of vampires, there is no official recognition of this fact. Even after a nest is cleaned out, town officials often deny there were ever any real vampires.

The underlying plot of the novel, though, is William Charles Felix's development into Jack's successor as leader of the slayers; in this sense it is a slayer initiation story. Felix, a rich young slacker, has drifted into amateur marihuana smuggling and then into running a bar. When Crow, whose life Felix saves during a drug shoot-out, recruits him to the team, Felix is stunned almost into catatonia by the vampires and outraged by Jack's warrior nihilism, which Felix sums up as "we're going to die anyway, so let's do it with style." After Crow's apparent death, Felix masterminds the killing of a particularly powerful master vampire—the first time it has ever been done—and accepts his destiny as leader of Team Felix. Crow has actually been turned into a vampire, and he pursues Felix to Rome, where he confronts his mentor and father figure, the Pope, whose touch is so holy it destroys him. The novel ends with Team Felix going off to do battle for God, and the Pope thinking "Oh Sweet Savior, how you must love them."

While Steakley's slayers are righteous if hard drinking and rambunctious, the vampires are post-human evil incarnate, self-proclaimed "gods" whose main pleasure seems to be degrading humans. While newer vampires ("goons") are little more than mindless, deadly animals driven by bloodlust, the older master vampires humiliate and brutalize humans before feeding on them. For Steakley, sexual debasement is worse than death, as it uses the victims' own desires against them; vampire sex is a perversion because one engages in it without real choice, reduced to a mere "wanton" object, addicted to the vampire as to a drug. Davette, who has been the sex toy of a master vampire, tells the team the story of her descent into degradation in excruciating detail, though the reader is largely spared the nasty particulars.

Steakley seems sincere in affirming equality and decency, but the real value put forward by the novel is the heroic self-sacrifice of the warrior, before which all other values pale. For Steakley, the thrill of combat and the risk of death for a righteous cause are the most intensely meaningful human experiences. His best writing emerges in the extended vampire fighting scenes, which are extraordinarily vivid; clearly the battle with virtually unbeatable opponents catches his imagination most strongly. Though the slayers risk death to save others, there is a certain morbidity in this eagerness to embrace the heroic, righteous death. Despite the theological framework, Steakley seems unable to convincingly affirm that the vampire slayers will get their reward in heaven; thus each death, if noble, is a tragic loss rather than meeting with the divine.

Most slayer stories not only affirm an ethos that harnesses violence for justice but imagine something beyond violence, such as truth or love. *Vampire$* harbors an emotional core of such incandescent rage at the loss of traditional value that the release of this anger through righteous violence and finally death is the only guiding principle. The normal world lacks significance; despite the affirmation of the love that develops between Felix and Davette or the spiritual righteousness embodied in the Pope, only the warrior's bond (and members of the team always know one when they see one), sealed in blood, really matters. As the vampires become the image of our world, degraded, greedy, self-indulgent, and effete, there is nothing but the slayer's death "with style" as the alternative to such corruption; in effect, it is the final proof of their contempt for, and superiority to, the vampires.

While *Near Dark* provides an image of a new dawn and a new life through its roots in the western, Steakley's revision of the Vietnam War story makes it hard for him to achieve the full affirmation he strives for; America's Vietnam War story is always unresolved. At the same time, the novel draws its force from the tension between allegiance to the doomed warrior and the Lamb of God, the anger at the corrupt contemporary world and the longing for tradition. What comes across most powerfully in *Vampire$* is the profound sense of a need for a framework of values to heal the vampire slayer's trauma and give the world order and meaning. While it does not engage in any postmodern irony, *Vampire$* clearly takes the crisis of the post-human moment seriously.

"My rage bordered on euphoria"

The above quotation comes from *Sunglasses after Dark,* the first book of Nancy Collins's *Midnight Blue* trilogy. [9] Sonja Blue, vampire/slayer is taken over by the Other, the predator self with which she shares her body; she has ceased to be Denise Thorne and become a living (rather than undead) vampire. The trilogy is about Sonja's struggle to come to terms with her divided and contradictory condition, a vampire but not dead, alive but not human. She becomes a vampire hunter, targeting first her monstrous sire, Lord Morgan, then all vampires, slaying with her deadly silver knife. The *Midnight Blue* series fuses the vampire story with the downbeat, violent cyberpunk version of the noir detective story found in Ridley Scott's *Blade Runner* and William Gibson's *Neuromancer*. Collins, though, substitutes for the relative nihilism characteristic of cyberpunk a mystical spirituality that finally transforms the future into a relative utopia. Though resolutely post-Christian, Collins's slayer story is a tale of both psychological and spiritual renewal in which therapeutic recovery is subsumed not simply in a quest for humane ethics and control over our innate violence but in a new spiritual realm provoked into existence by Sonja's relentless search for vengeance.

Unlike Caleb, Sonja cannot even imagine returning to the ordinary human world; Denise Thorne and all she represents are truly gone. Sonja is forever liminal, caught in eternal self-contradiction as the vampire who, as a vampire hunter, is always figuratively hunting herself. The post-human world she lives in doesn't appear to offer her a plausible home. *Midnight Blue* imagines a decadent, violent, vampire-ridden reality in which the human world is reduced to the status of illusion. Vampires magically cloak themselves with illusory appearances so humans can't perceive that their bodies are rotting corpses; only Sonja can adjust her vision so that she can see through their disguises. The streets of America are full of "Pretenders," the vampires, werewolves, ghosts, and other supernatural monsters ordinary people simply can't see. Religion has completely failed in *Sunglasses at Night,* which focuses on Sonja's battle with a corrupt faith healer who has telekinetic powers. Science is simply irrelevant, as it does not deal with the true nature of a reality that, despite the corruption of religion, is supernatural and spiritual.

Throughout the *Midnight Blue* series, Sonja's battles with the vampires are also about a woman's struggle with masculinity, particularly with father figures, both supernatural and human (when Sonja goes to her real father he rejects her), and with the power and violence they traditionally wield. Portions of the series depict a woman's fantasy of power over men who would hurt her, especially hurt her sexually; this is what Sonja's pursuit of Morgan is about, too, for he has raped her as well as drunk her blood, indifferently leaving her to die afterward. While Sonja is on a quest for vengeance, her story is also about an inner struggle to shape and accept an identity outside traditional femininity. Sonja has to settle accounts not only with those who have inflicted violence upon her but with her own attraction to, and pleasure in, violence; rage has become euphoric for her.

Her knee pistoned up, smashing into his denimed crotch and rupturing his testicles; it was as if a bomb had gone off in Rafe's jeans. He managed one high thin scream before collapsing. The agony of his ruined cojones was so great he didn't even know she'd fractured his pelvis.

The Blue Monkeys watched as Rafe spasmed on the floor, clutching his groin, their ape yell fallen silent.

That was when the Other made its move.

"You fuckers think you're tough, huh? You think you're bad? You shitheads can't even handle a girl!"

Shut up. Shut up. It's bad enough without you provoking them. Let's go. Let's just walk out of here damn you!

Two of them lunged at her, one from behind and one in front. The one behind grabbed her arms, pinning her elbows at her sides. The Other laughed and stamped on his instep, breaking it in two places. The Blue Monkey yowled and let go of her arms. The Other grabbed her frontal assault by the crotch and throat, lifting him off the floor.

No, stop. Please . . .

The Other tightened her grip on the boy's crotch. He made a bleating sound as she castrated him.

No. God, no. Stop . . .

She lifted the struggling youth over her head.

Don't!

The Other laughed as she hurled the boy against the wall. The sound his spine made as it snapped was delightful.

Someone swung a pool cue. She absorbed the blow across her back, although it cost her a couple of ribs. No big deal. Her laughter grew louder. The Other hadn't enjoyed herself so much in months.

Midnight Blue deals with the same issues as *Near Dark* in examining our instinctive attraction to violence and its pleasure, its drug-like "rush," as the Other clearly experiences it. As in Bigelow's movie, the pleasure of violence must be contained and given meaning, but Collins is willing to go further by portraying Sonja's truly ecstatic response to violence. While *Near Dark* contains violence within its affirmation of tradition and family, the *Midnight Blue* series has abandoned that possibility by setting the narrative in a cyber/noir world of the future. A return to family in any conventional sense is not an option for Sonja. It is in this context that Collins turns to supernaturalism in the form of a mythic apocalypse as the only way to salvation. The series grows into its mythical resolution; while *Sunglasses after Dark* is full of supernaturalism and religion, its tone is far more psychological, secular, and postmodern than the other two novels.

As she kills Morgan at the end of the trilogy, Sonja accepts that the Other is not really a second entity "hiding" within herself but a part of her identity. In an orgy of violence and supernatural transformation, Sonja becomes the "Queen of Nightmare," acknowledging both her desire for Morgan—as a father and a lover—and her need to kill him. In the end, she drinks his blood and her evolution is complete: "The Nightmare Queen began to sing her victory song, banging her sword against her shield as she danced on the body of her defeated foe. The faster she danced, the more intense the black fire surrounding Sonja's flesh became. Her ears were filled with the sound of drums and the clashing of swords and the ringing of bells. Flushed with victory and the exhilaration of birth, the newborn Destroyer touched down atop the World Trade Center and roared a challenge to the world." The romantic use of mythic archetypes and archaic imagery is balanced by the realism of the reference to the then-standing World Trade Center; Collins's supernaturalism seems genuine yet also self-consciously literary. Such an ending alone would leave Sonja whole but desolate, the Nightmare Queen and Destroyer, and Collins wants go beyond the nihilistic vision of the cyber/noir genre. In the course of hunting Morgan and killing vampires Sonja has become the surrogate mother of a child named Lethe, the product of Morgan's experiments in breeding humans with vampires. Lethe is the embodiment of the spiritual powers of evolution and the genesis of a new race—"Homo Mirablis"—who will be able to triumph over the evil Pretender races and the post-human world in which they thrive.

While Collins does affirm love and family, this isn't embodied in the traditional triad of mother-father-child, as in *Children of the Night;* Lethe mates with twenty-five men, bears sons, and moves on.

This supernaturalism provides a way out of the grim vision of a vampire-choked world where humans are either ignorant victims or pathetic willing servants of perverse and degenerate monsters; it transforms the apocalyptic reign of the vampires into vision of a better future. While Steakley's Catholic Church serves as a spiritual alternative, it represents the spiritual past rather than the future, a conserving, if not conservative, force that doesn't speak to contemporary women's needs. The supernatural Creator acting through Lethe in *Midnight Blue,* though derived from Jungian archetypes, is an imaginary faith, a pure fiction like King's "White Light" in *'Salem's Lot* or the glowing dawn that greets Caleb and Mae at the end of *Near Dark.* By shifting the resolution of Sonja's crisis of identity from a psychological realm to a mythic one, Collins creates images of both a healed identity and a healed world, transforming the violence and horror of the vampire into a cosmic love beyond romance or family. This new spirituality has a place for Sonja, since the Destroyer is the necessary compliment to Lethe, the Creator. *The Night Stalker, 'Salem's Lot, Near Dark, Vampire$,* and *Midnight Blue* testify to our need for an heroic figure and a myth of renewal, but they provide us with the shape of such a story, not its substance. As Kolchak says, it's a story; "believe it or not." All these slayer stories are a record of what is lost and can be recovered only in our imaginations.

The Slayers in Our Living Rooms

The Night Stalker, 'Salem's Lot, Near Dark, Vampire$, and *Midnight Blue* are each singular coherent narratives whose meaning is fully present in one story. However, two of the most important slayer stories of the 1990s are television series, which tell their stories in a completely different way. As with *Dark Shadows, Forever Knight* and *Buffy the Vampire Slayer* [10] are unfolding texts that develop over a course of television seasons through interaction with fans, changes in cast, crew, and writers, and the demands of television as a business. But unlike *Dark Shadows,* which aired daily installments of plots lasting weeks, *Forever Knight* and *Buffy* are weekly series in which each episode is a self-contained story as well as part of the larger series. While a single episode of *Dark Shadows* would probably be unintelligible, a single episode of *Forever Knight* or *Buffy* is typically a complete story.

This format means that *Forever Knight* and *Buffy* interact with both the medium and business of television and with the larger culture in a complicated way. Each new story uses the elements typical of its television genre—cop show or teen show—and, as is conventional for television, includes topical social issues as well. *Forever Knight* integrates Nick's quest to regain his humanity with traditional police story plots, including hunts for serial killers, witness protection stories, and hostage situations; therapy, politics, cults, television talk shows, AIDS, and virtual reality also appear in episodes. *Buffy's* characters worry about running for homecoming queen, selling band candy, performing in a talent show, trying out for cheerleader, having sex for the first time, and getting into college, as well as teenage suicide, runaways, and stalking.

Yet there are also continuing story lines that only make sense when one views a season, or the series, as a whole. No character is ever completely presented in a single episode; the writers often rely on a viewer's knowledge of details introduced in a previous episode or even a previous season. At the same time, motifs or characters that seemed important early on may disappear as the series develops; facts about characters may suddenly change. *Forever Knight* and *Buffy the Vampire Slayer* exist not as the sum of the individual episodes but as the sometimes-invisible total narrative, the meaning of which is never clear until the final episode.

While *Forever Knight* and *Buffy* have enjoyed success because television is fast becoming a niche rather than mass-market medium, a series still needs to command large audiences over a long period of time to succeed; television is also, even in the era of cable, significantly more cautious about its content than are movies or books. American television, particularly in drama, has a tradition of moral psychological realism, people making decisions about their lives in essentially personal and psychological terms. The dominant ethic of American television is rooted in an often simplified therapeutic model; one looks into oneself for what feels right, even in dealing with complex sociopolitical issues. Indeed, with its focus on personality and personal relationships, television has been an important force in affirming that ethics grow out of human psychology rather than external moral codes.

As fantasies focused on ethical issues, *Forever Knight* and *Buffy* negotiate between the ethics of psychological well-being and a world in which Good and Evil are external realities that impose upon us uncomfortable ethical duties. Because they are television series, *Forever Knight* and *Buffy* overtly endorse values that are more mainstream than a movie's or a novel's, but as vampire stories they are already outside the mainstream tradition of psychological realism and its sharp focus on the emotional lives of characters that typically leaves little room for the symbolic. Both series portray ethical choice as ambiguous, complex, and even dangerous—doing the right thing doesn't necessarily make one happy. *Forever Knight* is expressionistic and allegorical, though determinedly ambiguous about Nick's search for humanity; *Buffy* is both funnier and more overtly didactic. Both self-consciously exploit the line between mainstream television realism and the vampire story to speak to their audience.

"Poor Nicola, tortured by a soul he doesn't have"

In *Forever Knight,* the vampire, Nick Knight, is also a Toronto cop: "He was brought across in 1228," the introductory voice-over tells us, "preyed on humans for their blood. . . . Now he wants to be human again . . . repay society for his sins . . . to end his endless, forever night." [11] Nick's defining trauma is simply the fact that he is who he is. His vampire existence began to repulse him in the late eighteenth century; by the 1990s he has long since ceased to hunt humans, and his refrigerator is stocked with wine bottles filled with cows' blood. Nick is an addict in recovery; at one point he even tries a twelve-step program to deal with his need for blood. Nick belongs in the slayer category partly because in the pilot episode he stakes his vampire sire, La Croix. But the vampire Nick really wants to slay is himself, to cross back over the divide between human and post-human. The motif of slaying himself is literal; becoming human again will eventually lead to his death.

As played by Geraint Wyn Davies, Nick is the visual antithesis of the vampire: medium in size, he has dark blond hair and a pleasant, almost angelic, face (though Nick's often going unshaven makes the appearance more ambiguous than innocent). Of course he periodically "turns," at which point his eyes glow greenish-yellow, his fangs emerge, and he snarls like an animal. Nick is always reserved, distant, and cautious, a man keeping a secret; Davies portrays him as constantly hesitating before acting in any situation, overwhelmed by his secret existence, his memories, his guilt, and the duplicity they engender in him. As his vampire friend Janette says to him, their identities in the human world are only games they play until it is time to move on. While she finds this enjoyable, Nick has no core identity to confidently recognize as his own except the fundamental predatoriness he has rejected.

Yet as we see over and over, Nick already acts with humane values: he's reasonable, sensitive, and tolerant, with a strong empathy for suffering. Nick is an artist, both a painter and musician (he composed part of "Moonlight Sonata" for Beethoven), and as a cop he has channeled his predatory hunting instinct into protecting the public. His undead existence has made him aware of moral ambiguity and the ways humans and vampires alike are driven by need. No pragmatist, though, Nick cannot accept that acting human is the same as actually being human. He has an intensely guilty conscience and an acute sense of his own evil, his unquenchable thirst for blood, and the weight of his vampire past. Nick is a centerless post-human rebelling against his own condition, in search of the soul that Janette insists he does not have.

Each episode revolves around Nick's investigation of a crime that reminds him of an incident in his past, typically one in which he dealt with the realization that his existence as a vampire was wrong. While Edward Weyland in *The Vampire Tapestry* could never remember his previous lives, Nick is almost overwhelmed by his past, flooded with so many memories that he sometimes goes into a trance, a recollection of the past that erases his awareness of the present, and which the audience sees as a flashback. This device focuses viewers on the themes of the episode, asking them to consciously compare the two stories to find the common theme.

The producers and writers often acknowledge their relation to other vampire stories in circulation. In an episode entitled "Stranger than Fiction," Nick must protect the shy writer of Anne Rice–style vampire novels from a stalker. The other characters read her latest novel, and we see scenes of them imagining themselves in the story: Natalie as the vampire's lover

Nick Knight, Cop
(Geraint Wynn
Davies in the
television series
Forever Knight)

Nick Knight,
Vampire (Davies in
Forever Knight)

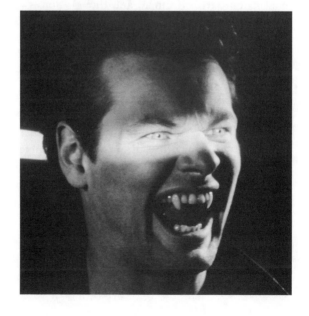

and Schanke, Nick's partner, as the master vampire. Self-consciously over-the-top, the scenes use the highly expressionist visual style (eccentric camera angles, rapid cutting, and extremely vivid, even garish color) the series typically uses to portray all events relating to vampires.

Forever Knight also gave post-human vampires a prominent place in the series. La Croix and Janette are ambiguous post-humans, not the enemy but a real alternative way of being. Though apparently slain by Nick, La Croix continues to appear in the flashbacks; and in the second season, he returns to his job as a late night talk radio host called "the Nightcrawler," announcing he is too old and powerful a vampire to be done in by a mere flaming stake in the heart. La Croix is obsessed with what he sees as Nicholas's betrayal of his "gift" of immortality, and throughout the series, he argues that Nick must put away his self-indulgent guilt and affectation of humanity. The elder vampire tells him to "be what you really are" and accept that his needs are his identity and his ethic. He often sends double-entendre messages to Nick on his radio broadcasts, to which Nick listens obsessively, unable to completely break with the "father" he once tried to kill.

Janette runs a vampire/leather bar called The Raven. The gaunt, deathly pale vampire is aggressively erotic in dress and manner, living only for her own satisfaction. She is content to be a vampire and constantly questions Nick's desire to be human, and though not as aggressive as La Croix in trying to bring Nick back to the old ways, she seems eager to renew their centuries-old intimacy. Nick does go to her sometimes for sex and comfort. La Croix and Janette are the ultimate insiders, sophisticated and sensual beings living a different kind of lifestyle, with no melancholy loneliness or sorrow about their condition. However, they are beyond any kind of ethical consciousness, and though they live for pleasure, La Croix seems to have no concept of happiness. Indeed, La Croix's arguments for being a pure predator are never really answered—simply rejected—and the sincerity of Janette's contentment as a vampire remains unchallenged for the first two seasons.[12]

When the series begins, Nick is already "passing" as human through sheer willpower fueled by self-revulsion. In the opening episode, a forensic pathologist named Natalie Lambert discovers Nick's secret when he wakes from presumed death in the morgue. Fascinated and tentatively attracted to him, Natalie tries to devise a medical cure for his "condition," as she

Cast of *Forever Night,* first season: Captain Stonetree (Gary Farmer), Natalie Lambert (Catherine Disher), La Croix (Nigel Bennett), Nick Knight (Geraint Wynn Davies, seated), Janette Duchame (Deborah Duchene), Don Schanke (John Kapelos).

insistently calls it. Thus, while Nick's desire to become human is often figured as a drama of sin and atonement, he is also portrayed as someone suffering from a disease that can be cured by science (though Natalie never confronts the question of how a blood disorder could enable Nick to fly). Nick remains skeptical that his problem is simply medical, for he experiences it as a deep spiritual trauma, knowing he has been a monster, an "irredeemable killer," as he calls himself in a moment of despair. Though Nick loves Natalie, or at least wants to love her, he can't commit to a relationship while he is still a vampire. Making love would mean drinking her blood, and he fears losing control and killing her. Nick has also learned that relationships with humans are, by his standards, short-lived; sometimes it seems that he simply can't share the intensity of Natalie's love as long as he is immortal. The good, scientific, wholesomely attractive Natalie is constantly contrasted to the amoral, exotic, erotic Janette; clearly neither love and neither world is right for Nick.

Nick's problems are also those of a new kind of man, as highlighted by the contrast with his first partner, Don Schanke, a crude, loud, but warm-hearted good old boy who often has trouble dealing with the way his life is going and the changes in the contemporary world. La Croix serves as the post-human form of new masculinity, a new barbarian who has put humanity aside as an absurdity. In addition to the father/son relationship, Nick's interaction with La Croix has obvious homoerotic overtones, which were occasionally played up by actor Nigel Bennett (La Croix wears considerably more eye makeup than either Janette or Natalie, particularly in the third season). Nick spends a good deal of time listening to Schanke, his surrogate brother, and La Croix, his father, expound their different philosophies, finding himself unable to identify with either.

At its best, the series refuses to resolve Nick's dilemma or reveal whether humanity and happiness can be obtained through science or love, by doing good or doing as one needs—even the definition of such terms is left unclear. We're clearly meant to identify with Nick, and we do so because he is caught between a traditional and a post-human form of identity, a vampire living as a human who wants spiritual and ethical answers to what our culture figures as psychological or medical problems. While we do not really want to see him become a vampire again, at times we want Nick to go back to Janette or reconcile with La Croix. The series seems skeptical that

Natalie's science, love, or human decency will ever help Nick achieve the humanity he seeks, though *Forever Knight* certainly relies on our anticipating romance between the two. This situation of uncertainty seems to go on forever, and while this is partly a dynamic of television storytelling, the writers of *Forever Knight* effectively turned this endless deferral of Nick's identity into their central theme.

During the third season, the producers decided to end the series. To a certain extent, what happened during the third season resulted from the demands of commercial storytelling, and one could see the conclusion of the series as a kind of meta-comment on how these demands tore the series apart. The truly savage ending includes all the other vampires and Tracy, Nick's new human partner, getting killed, with only La Croix, Nick, and Natalie left. In the final episode Nick and Natalie try to return Nick's humanity by letting him drink a little of her blood, but he is unable to restrain himself and she slips toward death; La Croix appears and suggests Nick bring her over; unwilling to condemn the woman he loves to endless, forever night, he lets her die. La Croix urges Nick to come with him, to accept his precious gift of life, but Nick affirms his love for Natalie and his faith in that love's power, demanding that La Croix kill him. La Croix fulfills Nick's wishes and has the final say: "Damn you, Nicholas." The series ends with an ambiguous shot of a red sun rising through the clouds.

Forever Knight is likely the only television series that ended by killing off all but one of the characters. The "scorched earth" finale sustains the ambiguity that was the keynote of the series. In effect, Nick becomes human, affirming love and commitment; but in doing so he embraces death. La Croix becomes the spokesman for life, affirming that it is a precious gift not to be thrown away. But to affirm life in La Croix's way is also to reject love, faith, connection. This ending also asserts that Nick's plight, caught among various versions of humanity, is the true image of the contemporary situation; there is no way out of the dilemma of the traumatized, post-human state, neither through therapy nor morality. In this, *Forever Knight* is like *Anno Dracula*, which accepts a postmodern world of endless partialness and fragmentation, where vampires and humans uneasily coexist as images of who and what humans are. What is striking about *Forever Knight* is not its resolution of the slayer/vampire story but the way, within the limits of a syndicated television series, it refuses the notion that there are easy or clear answers to what we mean by "humanity."

"I want to shop, date, hang out, go to school, save the world from demonic monsters. I want to do girly things."

After the shootings at Columbine High School in 1999, when WB delayed broadcast of two episodes of *Buffy the Vampire Slayer* because they were about violence in high schools, Sarah Michelle Gellar, who plays Buffy, issued the following statement: "I share the WB network's concern and compassion for the recent tragic events at Columbine High School and at academic campuses across the country. I am, however, disappointed that the year-long culmination of our efforts will not be seen by our audience. *Buffy the Vampire Slayer* has always been extremely responsible in its depiction of action sequences, fantasy and mythological situations. Our diverse and positive role models 'battle the horror of adolescence' through intelligence and integrity, and endeavor to offer a moral lesson with each new episode. There is probably no greater societal question we face than how to stop violence among our youth. By canceling intelligent programming like *Buffy the Vampire Slayer*, corporate entertainment is not addressing the problem." *Buffy* has an explicitly didactic intent within its commercial entertainment form. Buffy first appeared in a moderately successful feature film. Despite a fine performance by Kristy Swanson as Buffy, the movie *Buffy the Vampire Slayer* failed to take its own central idea—a contemporary high school girl confronted by monstrous evil—seriously enough. The series treats its vampires and demons as images of real evil and, even more importantly, treats the lives and problems of the human characters with the same seriousness.

Buffy the Vampire Slayer is arguably the best-written and most skillfully acted series on television, especially in the work of Gellar and Alyson Hannigan, who plays Willow Rosenberg, Buffy's best friend; the series also has a consistent and sophisticated visual quality. The scripts for individual episodes are so complex they are difficult to summarize, and this is especially true of the series' overall narrative. Producer Joss Whedon unobtrusively initiates story lines or character developments many episodes, even whole seasons, before they come to fruition. Further, in tracing out the serious themes of the series, one loses the sense of how clever and funny it is. *Buffy* is thus difficult to discuss in a short space, but the main outline of the series is clear.

Buffy the Vampire Slayer is set in Sunnydale, California, an archetypal American place like Las Vegas or 'Salem's Lot, and a suburban paradise of the post–World War II American dream. Though it's not a new idea that suburban paradise is actually an air-conditioned nightmare, Joss Whedon makes this motif literal; as Sunnydale is built on the "Hellmouth," it is infested with vampires and demons. Until the very end of the third season, none of the other students or their seldom-seen parents want to acknowledge this, despite the unusually high body count in the town and the high school; denial is simply the condition of suburban life. Even Buffy's mother, Joyce, doesn't realize Buffy is a slayer until the end of the second season. "What did you think when you washed the blood out of my clothes?" Buffy shouts when Joyce asks why Buffy never told her the truth. Because the series treats its tales of a young girl battling demons seriously, it became a vivid metaphor for the experience of adolescence in an American high school, then, when the characters graduated, for the situation of all young people in America.

Buffy is at its core an initiation story—Buffy and her friends are growing up and learning to be adults and most of the battles with supernatural monsters are metaphoric versions of ordinary teenage problems. The series works because it treats the interplay between the implied "real life" and the supernatural fantasy story, including its "girl power" version of feminism, with such texture and complexity. Though Buffy Summers, the "one girl in all the world to stand against the vampires and the demons" is not a vampire-slaying vampire, her status as the "Chosen One" makes her every bit as damaged an outsider as Nick Knight; like Nick, Buffy longs to be a normal human. Self-divided, living a secret life, Buffy is always caught between being Buffy the ordinary girl and Buffy the Vampire Slayer. The emotional core of *Buffy* is Buffy's loneliness as the Chosen One, the crushing responsibility she can't escape but learns to bear and finally to embrace. As played by Sarah Michelle Gellar, Buffy is small and fragile; though she has superhuman strength and can take a hit that would stop an elephant, her appearance accurately reflects her emotional state. Buffy not only has to find out how to be herself, as do all teenagers, but she has to accept a larger moral responsibility that requires sacrificing her own needs and desires and repeatedly risking her life.

Buffy is not literally alone; she has the aid of her "Watcher," Rupert Giles, the series' Van Helsing, who also becomes a father figure for her and her friends Willow Rosenberg and Xander Harris, the other two core characters of the series. A number of characters have come and gone; some, like Jenny Calandar and Kendra, have been killed, while others like Angel, Cordelia, Oz, and Riley have left under painful circumstances. Buffy longs for romantic love, and she has had relationships with Angel, a good vampire, and Riley, a demon-fighting soldier. Willow has felt an unrequited love for Xander and has shared relationships with Oz, a werewolf and musician, and Tara, a witch, though neither worked out. Xander has been involved with Cordelia Chase, the self-involved most popular girl in the school, a relationship that also failed. While these relationships are important to the characters and treated seriously, the core value of the series is not romantic love but friendship. The trio of Buffy, Willow, and Xander, who have been together since the first episode, is the heart of the series.

Even with support, Buffy is often on the verge of being overwhelmed by her responsibilities as slayer. Each season builds to a crisis in which Buffy has to make a choice to do the right thing even if it is dangerous or painful. At the end of the first season Buffy decides to face an especially powerful vampire known as "The Master," even though Giles finds a prophecy saying that she will die in this confrontation. Buffy does in fact die, but, resuscitated by Xander, she faces The Master a second time and destroys him. At the end of the second season, Buffy must send Angel to hell in order to avert the apocalypse; shattered, she runs away from Sunnydale to try to escape her responsibility as the slayer, eventually realizing she must go back.

As with any television series, *Buffy* relies on audience identification with the characters, but it also relies on the audience reading the stories as allegories for the overall themes. As a character-driven narrative, *Buffy* presents the problems the characters face in emotional and personal terms but also focuses on imagining contemporary life as a fragile series of ethical choices between Good and Evil in which the good often lose. It's not enough that the characters understand their own emotions and deal with them,

Buffy and friends, first season: Angel (David Boreanez), Buffy Summers (Sarah Michelle Gellar), Willow Rosenberg (Alyson Hennigan), Xander Harris (Nicholas Brendan, seated), Rupert Giles (Anthony Head), Cordelia Chase (Charisma Carpenter).

which is the typical happy ending in American television shows about teen-agers; they are always trying to grasp a larger moral purpose. When the brilliant Willow, who has been admitted to every college and university on earth, decides to stay in Sunnydale and go to the local branch of the University of California, she tells Buffy that it is because of not simply their friendship but also the chance to share in Buffy's continued struggle against evil. *Buffy* affirms that Good and Evil are not just matters of perspective, or even of a "healthy" way of being, but absolute values for which one should risk one's life.

Buffy is both a post-Christian story and a secular one; while Buffy wears a cross and uses holy water on vampires, no one ever invokes God, and the supernatural pastiche explaining the origins of vampires is never meant to create the kind of mythic aura of *Midnight Blue.* Yet the vampires and demons do establish the framework in which the idea of Good and Evil has imaginative force even without any theological underpinnings. In Buffy's world, cruelty, selfishness, self-indulgence, and indifference to others are figured not as mere psychological problems but as actual Evil. The ethical stance of the series emphasizes personal responsibility, respect for others, and compassion; the central ideal of the series is friendship. And if Evil is embodied in the vampires, Buffy has no corresponding image of transcendent Good to rely on; she has only herself and her humanly flawed companions.

Throughout the series, Buffy's battles with external evils are paralleled by her inward struggles with herself; her opponents are often her doubles or lovers. In the third season, Buffy encounters another slayer named Faith, who lives by the motto "Want-Take-Have," making her the slayer equivalent of the post-human vampire. Aggressive and reckless, Faith loves the violence of slaying and kills for pleasure; she is also sexually voracious, with a genuinely sadistic streak; in one episode she uses her superhuman strength to essentially rape Xander. It's made clear that Faith is as she is because of her traumatic childhood, but this is never presented as an excuse for her violence, only a reason. Finally Faith goes over to Evil and Buffy must fight her, a battle that leaves Faith in a coma. In the fourth season, Faith awakens and uses magic to switch bodies with Buffy, only to be defeated yet again. In the fifth season, Glory, a vicious, hyper-feminine god from another dimension, confronts Buffy with yet another avatar she must vanquish.

Return of the Slayer

On *Buffy the Vampire Slayer,* to be happy, to be good, to be truly human are difficult, endless pursuits. In one episode, depressed about how the vampires always come back, Buffy thinks to herself that because she will never win, her work is fruitless. "No fruit for Buffy," she says sadly. But she accepts that although Good will never actually triumph it is worth continuing to fight even for small and temporary victories against cruelty, violence, and fear. While such statements veer toward platitudes, the series gives it weight by making the suffering and loss experienced by the characters very real, as in the death of Buffy's mother. Few television series put their characters through as many changes as *Buffy*; Whedon seems to want the pace of their lives to match as closely as possible the pace of the lives of the viewers.

In the final episode of the fifth season, Buffy is faced once again with an intolerable choice. In order to defeat Glory, Buffy must kill her sister, Dawn. (Dawn is in fact a supernatural energy created in the form of a sister for Buffy, but as everyone now remembers Dawn as always having existed, she is de facto a real sister.) Buffy chooses to die herself rather than take her sister's life. Buffy's death is a release from the endless suffering of being a slayer, but it is also her final embrace of her heroic duty. Earlier, she has a vision in which she speaks with the mysterious "first slayer," who tells her that "death is your gift," meaning that the slayer brings death, that death is Buffy's release, but also that her death is the gift of life to Dawn and everyone she has saved.

What marks *Buffy the Vampire Slayer* as different from other slayer stories is its unambiguous affirmation not simply of the slayer but of her values. This endorsement is possible partly because, while *Buffy* accepts the reality of trauma and loss and the difficulty of becoming truly human, it always moves resolutely into the future. The characters are young, as is the intended audience. Their relationship to the heritage of the nineteenth century is attenuated; the Vietnam War, feminism, and the liberation movements of the sixties are not part of their experience. The post-human does not loom up before them as the alien future it is for older audiences; it is the reality they see around them all the time.

The acceptance of the future is acceptance of change; the characters affirm the future because they are constantly confronting it. The characters do not get better, or even more likable, nor do the relationships remain constant or smooth. On *Buffy the Vampire Slayer,* change is both endless and difficult. Taken as a whole, the series progresses from its original affirmation of the heroic slayer through an intentional naiveté in which youthful optimism and idealism, rather than a sense of the intractable burden of the lost past, are wedded to the fantasy of heroism. By the fifth season, the series darkens considerably, with a stronger sense of mortality and the price of heroism shadowing its optimism. *Buffy* balances an ethos rooted in individual psychology with the demands of a world in which Good and Evil exist as absolutes. Optimism and idealism are counter-weighed with an acute sense of mortality and suffering. This complex balance and the difficult shading it requires allow *Buffy* to both affirm an ethical position and accept the reality of death. Though Buffy is resurrected so the series can continue, Whedon recognized that this slayer could not really be the Chosen One until she had accepted fully her fate and lived out the implications of her own mortality. Because Buffy dies in the one-hundredth episode, she is the vampire slayer who takes back the future from the demons and returns it to humanity.

Buffy (Sarah Michelle Gellar) armed with a stake and ready to slay.

Conclusion

THE PERSISTENCE
OF LEGEND

I know that I appear to have created an allegory for the imaginative and
ethical history of our era, taming the vampire story by tracing the movement from vampire protagonist to the post-human to the return of the
slayer. But the history of the vampire story is not really so neat. After all,
*Child of the Night, Vampire$, Dracula: The Norton Critical Edition, Nadja,
Anno Dracula,* and *Buffy the Vampire Slayer* all appear at virtually the same
moment; none dominates the others as the current vampire story. Nor do
earlier vampire stories disappear simply because my argument moves on
from them. While the structure of this book gives the impression that the
slayer has replaced the vampire as the object of our interest and identification, it simply reflects my own fantasies and aspirations, the mythographer
unable to resist mythologizing. The slayer has simply returned; the vampire protagonist—the alienated, sensitive, passionate stranger with the unquenchable thirst—remains a potent figure. The liberated vampire, the
post-human vampire, and the slayer continue in a dynamic interchange as
their coexistence gives depth and complexity to each other. The central
ethical term in this book—"human"—thus remains in a state of flux, undefined. The variety of vampire stories is a sign of the cultural complexity
or, maybe more honestly, incoherence articulated in these tales, not of our
progress.

At the beginning of this book I wrote that these stories not only participate in a conversation about our culture in mindful ways but reflect a new condition of meaning. We may always feel unsure about the meanings we find in *Near Dark* or *Midnight Blue* or *'Salems' Lot* because these meanings have no support but our own temporary choice to assent to them, but this uncertainty seems increasingly to color all meaning, all forms of understanding. How does meaning arise in these works? We find it by paying careful attention, reading and watching in a way that is attuned to significance as well as entertainment, rhetoric as well as pleasure. Meaning, however, is not merely the accidental by-product of our attention but something that exists in the work itself. Though I hope I have paid adequate respect to the seriousness of purpose and skill among these writers, filmmakers, and television producers, I don't assign meaning to the realm of genius and the revelation of eternal truths. Meaning is not the same as a completely coherent or true vision.

In some instances meaning emerges, perhaps unexpectedly, out of a struggle with the inner dynamics of the vampire story, the conditions of the medium in which an artist works, or the demands of the market at that moment. In other instances a particular artist or group of performers and writers impress upon the material the point of view that they bring to the vampire story. The Hammer filmmakers and *Dark Shadows* producers and writers discovered meaning in the collision of entertainment with circumstances in the entertainment business and the larger culture. Steven King, Anne Rice, Chelsea Quinn Yarbro, Kim Newman, Abel Ferrera and Nicholas St. John, and others approached the vampire story with a point of view to express, but circumstances of genre, medium, and culture then reshaped that expression.

In the end, these factors are in play all the time, and there is no rule by which the relation between them and authorial intent can be established. Such a situation leads me to think that meaning can best be understood as the result of the interaction of institutional and cultural circumstances, such as the production of commercial entertainment, with the human work of expression and communication. In these stories, meaning is the mark left by the work of imagination, the engagement with the specific materials and possibilities of the vampire story. If in the end each of these works comes to a point where its articulation of meaning turns into paradox, ambiguity, inconsistency, or even contradiction, that is part of the condition of such meaning.

The meaning that emerges from any of these works, however much they focus on ethical themes and issues, is not a prescription for action. Unlike self-help books, these stories are not tools, for we can be vampires or slayers only in our fantasies; if vampire stories are not immediately graspable tools for living they are also not reliable guides to the nature of reality. Rather, like all fictions, vampire stories define a range of imaginative sensibilities in which ideas and thoughts are fused with a way of experiencing them. Meaning, at least in an artistic sense, is better understood as an aspiration to understanding rather than a revelation. At the same time, these stories fulfill our desire to escape from our fears into the imaginary world where terror takes on the benign shape of entertainment and comes back to us as pleasure, but this is also part of their meaning, not a barrier to it. My point has not been that we must learn Great Truths from these stories—though, as I have said, some people, myself included, find important truths in them—but that we should share in the aspiration to meaning that these works embody.

It is a measure of the materialistic, power-obsessed quality of our culture that such things as sensibility, attitude, and aspiration seem vague and wispy, without immediate instrumentality or practical value. In an era of science and the furious pursuit of reality in the forms of fact, technology, and power, the vampire story brings us a version of something we lack, a sense of the inexplicable and mysterious, of the possibility that not everything can be known and controlled. Fantasy has about it the quality of adolescence and immaturity, but "fantasy" originally meant "to make visible," and this is what these stories do: for good and bad, they make visible a way of understanding the world that accepts the limits of understanding.

But I don't think of these stories as simply meta-fictions about the nature of meaning. They actually make contributions to our way of understanding the issues that I have identified as central to them. They enter into a particular version of a search for an understanding of human nature, ethics, and our relation to the past that was going on for at least two centuries before it became part of the vampire story, and which was going on in more "serious" forms even as it was addressed in tales of vampires and slayers. One could perhaps try to draw all these conversations together into one vast synthesis, but it seems equally important to realize that the creation of meaning occurs simultaneously in a variety of venues and registers that overlap but that are also disparate, arising in different languages and circumstances, addressing different audiences. These different meanings may never come together to form a synthesis; certainly for all their commonality, vampire stories remain intractably different from each other.

The limits of these stories are obvious. For all their daring and exoticism, vampire stories don't strike me as particularly radical; when we see them as subversive we are responding to the vampire's style and celebrity status more than the core values the stories wrestle, traditional values of freedom, heroism, love, the family, and friendship. At the same time, they articulate those values in a variety of ways and, as they imagine a world different from our own, provide a lens through which we can re-envision it. In a world in which no story or group of stories can be expected to encompass all possible meanings, all forms of truth and value, we gain most if we focus on what these stories accomplish even as we understand their inescapable limits.

These stories clarify the tensions and commonalties between our various ideas of humanity, ethics, and our relation to tradition. By exploring these ideas in stories of the mysterious, dangerous, and terrifying, we gain a sense of how deeply resonant these issues are for us. At the core of the vampire story's significance for us is our nightmare struggle with hopelessness and fear, the sense that we are prey to forces beyond us, feelings that are particularly powerful, if often suppressed, in late-twentieth-century America. At the height of American power and prosperity we find that we have made our world less satisfying than it should be, and though Americans have a poor record of articulating such uncertainties, the vampire story accomplishes some of that for us.

These works make clear the ambiguity and incoherence that underlies any ethical position, offering as they do incomplete attempts to make a coherent whole; these stories not only offer a center of value but define the boundaries of our search for such a center. They show us that we cannot understand reality without fantasy and cannot create a future except from the images of the past. Perhaps most significant, these stories make clear how important both ethics and imagination are to our sense of identity and purpose. Fiction serves as a way of understanding our world by imagining it in new forms, and the choices we make about ethics go as deeply to the core of our being as such elemental forces as sex and violence. Though these stories prove or settle nothing, by their existence they ultimately affirm not simply the impulse to liberation or the need for self-control, the power of violence or sexuality, but imagination itself, the use of the unreal to order reality in a meaningful way. By creating stories out of fear and hopelessness we remind ourselves about the powers and limitations of our own imaginations to deal with them.

Schooled as I have been in the academic values of skepticism and proof and the literary value of irony, I sometimes find the idealism of many of these stories, their affirmation of the soul, humanity, and transcendence far harder to accept than their sensationalism or their violence. In my role as academic Van Helsing, I am part of the world of demystification and disenchantment, and however much I am attracted to these stories, I bring to them a suspicion about their supernatural fantasies and their appeal to what we want to believe in, their faith in symbols and imagination. But the aspirations for freedom and liberation, for a moral standard to live by, for heroism, for friendship and community are fundamental human desires. These desires, in whatever shapes they take, whether dreams or nightmares, remind us of not only this fact but how essential it is to imagine and articulate them. Perhaps I should understand myself less through the image of Van Helsing, that certain and righteous scientist of the vampire, than through Nick Knight and Buffy Summers, slayers whose battle with the vampire never ends and who are not always sure what is right.

Thus this book ends with the vampire unslain, the slayer still hunting, the themes and issues addressed in these novels, movies, and television series unresolved. Like any vampire story, this book looks uncertainly into a future I cannot predict. Saint-Germain will have new adventures, *Buffy the Vampire Slayer* will go on, and Barnabas Collins's, Sonja Blue's, and Nick Knight's stories will continue to circulate; perhaps they too will come back for new stories at some point. As both the nineteenth century's heritage and our current urgency about shaping an ethic of humanity for the new century recede, perhaps new themes and motifs will be integrated into the vampire story so they remain a dynamic part of our culture. Vampires might become a fiction we no longer believe in, a relic of a curious turn in the late-twentieth-century imagination, or simply vanish.

In *The X Files* episode *Bad Blood*, the vampire sheriff tells Agent Scully that it's not like it used to be; "we're good citizens, good neighbors now." Roy, a pathetic pizza delivery boy with plastic fangs who longs to be Dracula, and who Mulder and Scully are pursuing, just didn't, the sheriff says, "understand the meaning of low profile." Perhaps that is the vampires' fate, to fade into a low profile, becoming cultural and imaginative good citizens, absorbed into a comic episode of another genre; if they do, they will also force the slayer into retirement. To hold onto Stoker's *Dracula* or any vampire story as a classic or as "our story" is a natural human impulse, for then it can serve as one small fixed point in the reality of change without end, but that is the route to keeping a low profile. To be a dynamic part of the life of our moment, to undergo complex change and give that change imaginative meaning, even at the cost of sometimes appearing lurid, sensationalist, adolescent, and even silly, is what becomes a legend most.

NOTES

Introduction

1. The vampire encyclopedias include J. Gordon Melton, *The Vampire Book: The Encyclopedia of the Undead;* Matthew Brunson, *The Vampire Encyclopedia;* Manuela Dunn Mascetti, *Vampire: The Complete Guide to the World of the Undead;* and David J. Skal, *V is for Vampire.*

2. David Pirie, *A Heritage of Horror* and *Vampire Cinema.* For a good bibliography of vampire novels, movies, and plays, see both editions of J. Gordon Melton, *The Vampire Book: The Encyclopedia of the Undead* (Detroit: Visible Ink, 1997, 1999).

3. Not only are the original episodes rerun; the fan club continues to operate and hold conventions at which the actors and writers appear.

4. Critical books on vampire stories include: James B. Twitchell, *The Living Dead: A Study of the Vampire in Romantic Literature,* which, as the title says, approaches the vampire as an aspect of romantic literature, placing a strong emphasis on a psychoanalytic approach; Alain Silver and James Ursini's *The Vampire Film* is a shrewd survey from a formalist perspective emphasizing shifting conventions and motifs in the vampire film; Gregory Waller, in *The Living and the Undead,* focuses on vampires of the twentieth-century from Stoker through Romero's *Dawn of the Dead,* obviously dealing with zombies and other monsters from the grave; Nina Auerbach, *Our Vampires, Ourselves,* takes a feminist political approach to the history of the vampire story, emphasizing its sensitivity to sexual politics and larger political realties such as the Reagan presidency. Auerbach is a perceptive observer of the details of vampire stories, though on occasion I find her readings of the changes in the vampire story too sweepingly allegorical of large-scale political and social trends. Recent critical work includes Laurence A. Rickels, *The Vampire Lectures.* Three anthologies of criticism have also appeared the wake of the hundredth anniversary of the publication of *Dracula:* Joan Gorden and Veronica Hollinger,

Blood Read: The Vampire as Metaphor in Contemporary Culture; Carol Margaret Davison and Paul Simpson-Howley, *Bram Stoker's Dracula: Sucking through the Century 1897–1997;* and Leonard G. Heldreth and Mary Phar, *The Blood Is the Life: Vampires in Literature.* Patricia Altner's *Vampire Readings: An Annotated Bibliography* is a bibliography of critical writing about vampires.

    5. Auerbach, *Our Vampires, Ourselves,* 6.

Chapter 1: Vampire History

    1. Anthologies of vampire stories are often historical, such as Alan Ryan, ed., *Vampyres: Two Centuries of Great Vampire Stories;* Christopher Frayling, ed., *Vampyres;* and Richard Dalby, ed., *Dracula's Brood.* Popular histories of the vampire include such works as Basil Copper, *The Vampire in Legend, Fact, and Art,* and Clare Haworth-Maden, *The Essential Dracula.*

    2. For a useful source on the vampire in folklore and history, see Gabriel Ronay, *The Truth About Dracula.*

    3. The single most famous "real" vampire case was that of Arnold Paul in Austro-Hungarian Serbia, who claimed to have been attacked by a vampire while fighting the Turks. He died in 1727, and soon people reported that he had risen from the grave as a vampire and begun attacking people. Paul and the others who had died recently were exhumed, beheaded, and burned. A second wave of vampire attack reports in 1731 was attributed to the eating of meat from vampirized cows. The case was investigated by Austro-Hungarian military doctors, who took it quite seriously (though calling an early-eighteenth-century army doctor a scientist is something of a stretch), and became the basis for much of the work of Don Augustine Calumet, a French vampire investigator who left the issue of vampires' existence open.

    4. The materials of the debate have been summarized by Montague Summers, an Anglican minister who became a Roman Catholic priest. He took all of these accounts completely seriously and saw it as his duty to warn people against the very real dangers of vampires in his books *The Vampire: His Kith and Kin* (n.p., 1928) and *The European Vampire* (n.p., 1929). Summers was obviously an eccentric, out of step with his time, and such books could easily be read as superstitious nonsense.

    5. Noreen Dresser, *American Vampires.* See also: Karyn Zweifel, *Southern Vampires,* which mixes fiction with "real vampire" interviews; Carol Page, *Bloodlust: Conversations with Real Vampires;* and Katherine Ramsland, *Piercing the Darkness: Undercover with Vampires in America Today.*

    6. I should make clear that I am essentially a strict constructionist in determining what is and what isn't a vampire story. George Romero's brilliant *Night of the Living Dead* and its two sequels are zombie movies. Dan Simmons's terrifying *Carrion Comfort* (New York: Warner Books, 1989) is about creatures with telepathic powers, even if they are called psychic "vampires." While vampires often have telepathic powers, in this novel vampirism is invoked only as a metaphor to define beings that have no other name. In David Cronenberg's *Rabid* (1977), Marilyn Chambers's character has a disease that has caused her body to mutate, but

she is not a vampire, despite parallels with Murnau's *Nosferatu*. These are fine stories, but they are not vampire stories.

7. D.L. MacDonald's *Poor Polidori* gives the fullest account of the writing and reception of the "The Vampyre."

8. Tom Holland, *Lord of the Dead.*

9. Auerbach and Twitchell provide substantial accounts of the nineteenth-century vampire; the anthology *Vampires, Wine, and Roses,* ed. John Richard Stephens, provides a number of examples of nineteenth-century vampires. Twitchell argues that "Carmilla" is a completion of "Christabel."

10. James Malcolm Rymer's *Varney the Vampire; or The Feast of Blood* was reprinted in 1970, ed. Devendra P. Varma, and in 1972, ed. E.F. Blieler. Treated as a novel, *Varney* is virtually unreadable. He's not even a very effective vampire, as he is usually interrupted during his feeding when the victim cries out for help.

11. On *Dracula,* see: Leonard Wolf's *The Essential Dracula;* Clive Leatherdale's *Dracula: The Novel and the Legend* and *The Origins of Dracula,* which compiles essays thought to have influenced Stoker; Carol Senf's *Dracula: Between Tradition and Modernism;* Elizabeth Miller, ed., *Dracula: The Shade and the Shadow.* David J. Skal's *Hollywood Gothic: The Tangled Web of Dracula from Stage to Screen* is invaluable. On Dracula movies, see James Craig Holte, *Dracula in the Dark.* Gregory Waller's *The Living and the Undead,* which deals with twentieth-century vampires as well as Romero's zombies and other monsters from the grave, offers an intelligent and shrewd reading of *Dracula* as a tale of moral community. For those interested in the historical Dracula, a.k.a. Vlad the Impaler, see Raymond MacNally and Radu Florescu, *In Search of Dracula.*

12. *Nosferatu,* dir. F.W. Murnau, Prana Films, 1922; *Vampyr,* dir. Carl Fryer, Tobia-Klangfilm, 1932. Florence Stoker's suit caused Murnau's film to be withdrawn, and supposedly all prints were destroyed by Universal after they bought the rights to the play.

13. Both *Nosferatu* and *Vampyr* suffer from looking creaky today. At times, Murnau sped up the film so that Orlock appears to move very fast, and this technique isn't effective, partly because of the convention that—if one is not going to use rapid cutting—slow motion is scary motion. Regarding Dryer's movie, symbolism and unreality are no longer the idiom by which we represent dreams and nightmares, though portions of *Vampyr* remain quite scary. Although both remain important as films by major directors, or as silent classics, only Murnau's movie survives as a dynamic part of the vampire story, and then only through Werner Herzog's 1979 revision.

14. *Dracula,* dir. Tod Browning, Universal, 1931.

15. Auerbach argues that Lugosi's Count is humanized, and while this is true in the sense that we see no fangs or other evidence of animalism, the aura of the strange, rooted in Lugosi's accent, and the supernatural is a powerful part of his presence.

16. As is often noted, the Spanish language version, shot on the same sets while the American company was off duty, is more explicit about the sexual quality of the vampire (though to contemporary eyes the differences, while real, seem rather

innocent), but even here the focus is on the Count as dangerous seducer rather than as power-mad monster.

17. *Dracula* and *Frankenstein* were released again in 1968 to art and revival houses after *Dark Shadows* and the Hammer *Dracula* movies helped renew public interest in the vampire story.

18. See Skal, *Hollywood Gothic,* for a full discussion of this history. In 1968, the PBS station in Cleveland ran a festival of the Universal movies hosted by Don Robertson, a local journalist and novelist who was an important influence on Stephen King. Even this retrospective treated the movies largely as fascinating antiques.

19. *Horror of Dracula,* dir. Terence Fisher, Hammer Films, 1958.

20. Hammer had been in existence in one form or another since the mid-1930s; it was a very successful business through the early 1970s. The Hammer attitude is summed up in Christopher Lee's comment "Hammer has never claimed to be here for anything other than to provide the general cinema-going public with the entertainment it wants. That is, of course, the job of the showman. . . ." *House of Horror: The Complete Hammer Films Story,* ed. Jack Hunter (1973; Rev. ed., London: Creation Books, 1994), 23. From the beginning of the series, Hammer had releasing deals with American studios and was always concerned with the American market. Hammer movies in the United States were directed largely at the teenage audience, and while they appealed to a young audience in Britain too, there was a distinct sense that they were also working-class entertainment.

21. Hunter, ed., *House of Horror,* 18.

22. There had been European versions of the Carmilla story, such as the Spanish film *The Blood Spattered Bride,* earlier in the decade.

23. Peter Hutchings, *Hammer and Beyond: The British Horror Film.*

24. In 1959 Cushing played Sherlock Holmes in Hammer's *Hound of the Baskervilles,* and he plays Holmes and Van Helsing as very similar characters.

25. *Once Bitten,* dir. Howard Storm, Goldwyn, 1985; *Vamp* dir. Richard Wenk, New World/Balcor, 1986. For particularly interesting commentary on these movies, see Silver and Ursini, *The Vampire Film.*

26. *Fright Night,* dir. Tom Holland, Columbia, 1985.

27. Tom Holland, the writer and director, also wrote *Lord of the Dead,* the novel about Byron as vampire.

28. The sequel, *Fright Night 2,* pursues the theme of scary female sexuality when a female vampire named Regine goes after Charley and Peter.

29. *The Lost Boys,* dir. Joel Schumacher, Warner Brothers, 1987.

30. *Def By Temptation,* dir. James Bond III, Orpheus/Bonded Filmworks/Troma, 1990.

31. Poppy Z. Brite, ed., *Love in Vein.*

32. Ibid., x.

Chapter 2: The Vampire Liberation Front

1. *Dark Shadows,* Dan Curtis Productions, 1966–1971. Kathryn Leigh Scott, ed., *The Dark Shadows Companion,* is invaluable for information about the series.

Scott played Maggie Evans in the original series, and the book contains essays and recollections from many of the cast and crew members.

2. The importance of niche marketing can't be overestimated in the popularity of the vampire story. Niche marketing can restore the communicative relationship between artist and audience, as they can now be assumed to speak a common language that is not simply the language of the largest possible audience. The variety of vampire stories, particularly those marketed in novel series, is directly related to the ability of authors to identify and address particular audiences, often through small independent publishers such as Lucard ("Dracul" spelled backwards), White Wolf, and Living Batch Press. Tor, which also publishes a variety of fantasy, horror, and science fiction novels, is also an important publisher of such vampire lore as S.P. Somtow's Valentine trilogy and Brian Lumley's Necroscope novels. Many of these novels are among the best in the genre: White Wolf publishes Nancy Collins's *Midnight Blue Trilogy;* and Living Batch publishes Charnas's *Vampire Tapestry,* which was originally a Simon and Schuster book.

3. Despite these stories and the appearance of Quentin, the werewolf member of the Collins family, played by the very handsome and popular David Selby in the fourth season, *Dark Shadows* always remained "the vampire soap opera."

4. *Blacula,* dir. William Crain, American International Pictures, 1972.

5. In 1970 the theatrical movie *House of Dark Shadows,* far more violent than the television series, was released by MGM. In addition to the cinema's greater openness to violence, the movie's need for a decisive conclusion led Curtis and the writers back to their original conception of the vampire: Barnabas is evil and is finally killed. *House of Dark Shadows* was clearly in line with the Hammer vampire movies to which critics compared it, though the visual style was quite different. The movie did well at the box office, but the ratings for the television series began to decline. Frid has suggested that the movie version broke the spell of the "never-never land" quality of the series. Though this is true, the movie broke with something more important: the unique quality of Barnabas as protagonist. As a variant of Hammer's Dracula, Barnabas lost his status as the character who stood for the audience. When Barnabas disappeared from the series and Frid became Bramwell, the central focus of the series, the vampire, was also gone.

6. Anne Rice, *Interview with the Vampire* (New York: Alfred A. Knopf, 1976).

7. On the world of Anne Rice fans, see Jana Marcus, *In the Shadow of the Vampire: Reflections from the World of Anne Rice,* which includes interviews with fans and photos from the Memnoch Ball in New Orleans. Other works on Rice include Gary Hoppenstand and Ray Browne, eds., *The Gothic World of Anne Rice,* and Katherine Ramsland, *The Vampire Chronicles: The Official Guide to Anne Rice's* The Vampire Chronicles. Ramsland has also written *Prism in the Night: A Biography of Anne Rice.*

8. Anne Rice, *The Vampire Lestat* (New York: Alfred A. Knopf, 1985).

9. Anne Rice, *The Queen of the Damned* (New York: Alfred A. Knopf, 1988).

10. Chelsea Quinn Yarbro, *Hotel Transylvania* (New York: St. Martin's Press, 1978); *The Palace* (New York: St. Martin's Press, 1978); *Blood Games* (New York: St. Martin's Press, 1981).

11. This secrecy changes in *Out of the House of Life*, in which Saint-Germain tells of his early life in a series of letters to Madeleine de Montalia, now a vampire archeologist, who is on a dig at the site of these events.

12. P.N. Elrod, *Bloodlist* (New York: Ace Books, 1990).

13. An example of these two impulses yoked together is Christopher Pike's *The Last Vampire*, in which the vampire Alisa Perne, also know as Sita (her name changes when she becomes a vampire five thousand years ago), is an image of complete freedom—powerful, without the slightest shame or guilt about sex or violence—and at the same time searching for both romance and spiritual love. She eventually becomes human again, but early in the series these two sides of her simply coexist. Written primarily for a young audience, the desire for both freedom and love needs to be embodied in the vampire/narrator.

14. George R.R. Martin, *Fevre Dream* (New York: Doubleday & Co, 1982).

15. *Sundown: the Vampire in Retreat*, dir. Anthony Hickox, Verston, 1990.

16. *Kindred: The Embraced*, Aaron Spelling Productions, 1996.

17. Michael Romkey, *I, Vampire* (New York: Ballantine, 1990).

18. Jewelle Gomez, *The Gilda Stories* (Ithaca: Firebrand Books, 1991).

19. Nancy Kilpatrick, *Child of the Night* (Nottingham, Great Britain: Pumpkin Books, 1996).

Chapter 3: The Dracula Variations: Part I

1. *Blood for Dracula*, dir. Paul Morrissey and (uncredited) Anthony Dawson, CC Champion/Jean Yanne-Jean Pierre Rassam/Warhol Productions, 1993. The Criterion DVD of *Blood for Dracula* is an invaluable resource, including commentary by both Paul Morrissey and Udo Kier.

2. Fred Sabgerhagen, *The Dracula Tape* (1975; Reprint, New York: Tor, 1989).

3. *Love at First Bite*, dir. Stan Dragoti, Simon Productions/American International Pictures, 1979; *Dracula*, dir. John Badham, Universal Studios, 1979; *Bram Stoker's Dracula*, dir. Francis Ford Coppola, Columbia/Zoetrope/Osiris, 1992.

4. Auerbach sees attempts to make Dracula romantic as strange and bizarre. While I agree that nothing in Stoker's Count really suggests romance, by the 1970s, Stoker was so thoroughly mixed with Lugosi, Lee, and the rest that this transformation was more or less inevitable.

Chapter 4: Post-Human Vampires: "We Are Animals"

1. *Martin*, dir. George Romero, Braddock Associates/Libra/Laurel Group, 1976; *Nosferatu*, dir. Werner Herzog, Herzog/Gaumont, 1979; Whitley Strieber, *The Hunger* (New York: William Morrow & Co., 1981); *The Hunger*, dir. Tony Scott, MGM, 1983; Suzy McKee Charnas, *The Vampire Tapestry* (New York: Simon and Schuster, 1981); *Vampire's Kiss*, dir. Robert Bierman, Hemdale, 1989; *Habit*, dir. Larry Fessenden, Glass Eye Pix, 1997; *The Addiction*, dir. Abel Ferrera, October Films, 1995.

2. Strieber, *The Hunger*, 306.

3. Barbara E. Hort, *Unholy Hungers: Encountering the Psychic Vampire in Ourselves and Others* (Boston: Shambala, 1996).

4. *Najda*, written and directed by Michael Almeredya, could be included in this section, for like *The Addiction* and *Habit* it presents the vampire through the conventions of the urban horror story and uses a New York City setting; but it is also a Dracula variation, so I have chosen to include it in the next chapter.

5. I was raised a Catholic, so Ferrera and St. John's theology was very familiar to me; the Presbyterian and Jewish friends with whom I saw the movie were more than a little baffled.

Chapter 5: The Dracula Variations: Part II

1. Kim Newman, *Anno Dracula* (New York: Carroll and Graf, 1992); Dan Simmons, *Children of the Night* (New York: G.P. Putnam, 1992); Marie Kiraly, *Mina* (New York: Berkley, 1994); Roderick Anscombe, *The Secret Life of Lazlo, Count Dracula* (New York: Hyperion, 1994); *Nadja*, dir. Michael Almereyda, October Films, 1994.

2. In addition to *Anno Dracula*, as with many successful vampire novelists, Newman has produced a series of novels that take place in the same world, including *The Bloody Red Baron* and *Judgment of Tears: Anno Dracula 1959*. In the final novel Dracula dies, though vampires live on.

3. I have been genuinely unsure about whether it was more useful to look at *Nadja* through the lens of the post-human story or as a Dracula variation. Its position at this point in the chapter is an acknowledgment that it is both.

4. Leonard Woolf's *The Essential Dracula*, part of a series including *Frankenstein* and *Dr. Jeykll and Mr. Hyde*, is an annotated edition that can be used in the classroom, but it is not strictly speaking a scholarly/teaching edition in the way the Norton is. Further, the Norton Critical Editions are an immense, ongoing publishing project for a company with a powerful say of what is canonical and what is not.

5. *Dracula: A Norton Critical Edition*, ed. Nina Auerbach and David Skal (New York: W.W. Norton & Co., 1997).

Chapter 6: Return of the Slayer

1. *Alien* (1979), *Aliens* (1982), *Alien 3* (1992), and *Alien Resurrection* (1997). Particularly in the last two movies Sigourney Weaver had a good deal of say in how Ripley was portrayed; although Ripley has been a very attractive character for women, the screenwriters and directors were all men, so she is also a figure in men's reimagining of gender, heroism, and identity.

2. *The Night Stalker*, Dan Curtis Productions, 1972. The movie had been out on video in the 1980s and was first reissued on video; then, on DVD in 1998. The movie spawned a television series of the same name in which the hero, perpetually harried and bedraggled reporter Carl Kolchack, was constantly running into trouble with the authorities as well as the zombies, witches, rakshasas, diableros,

headless bikers, aliens, and other monsters that passed through Chicago. *The Night Stalker* series in turn provided an important inspiration for Chris Carter's *The X-Files*, the archetypal conspiracy story of the 1990s. The television series also runs occasionally on the SciFi Channel. Its revival is attributable to the interest in vampire stories and perhaps to Darren McGaven's appearances on the *X-Files* and *Millennium*, also a Chris Carter series.

3. Stephen King, *'Salem's Lot* (New York: Doubleday, 1976).

4. The 1979 television miniseries of the novel solves the Susan problem in the way the novel implies but doesn't follow through on; she becomes a vampire and Ben and Mark must stake her.

5. *Near Dark*, dir. Kathryn Bigelow, DEG/Feldman-Meeker, 1987.

6. *Near Dark* isn't the first vampire Western; the interesting *Curse of the Undead* (1959) and uninteresting *Billy the Kid Meets Dracula* (1966) precede it.

7. This is essentially Auerbach's point of view, focusing on the power of the father to set things right as well as the film's affirmation of family.

8. John Steakley, *Vampire$* (New York: Penguin, 1990).

9. *Sunglasses after Dark* was published in 1992; *In the Blood,* in 1993; *Paint It Black,* in 1994. All are published together in the White Wolf Press book *Midnight Blue: The Sonja Blue Collection* (1995).

10. *Forever Knight,* Pargon Productions, 1992–95. *Buffy the Vampire Slayer,* Kuzui Productions, 1997–present.

11. In 1989, CBS broadcast a pilot film called *Nick Knight, Vampire Cop,* starring Rick Springfield, produced and written by James Parriot and Barney Cohen. The series didn't materialize until 1992, as a syndicated show made in Canada in cooperation with German television. The original movie, reshot with the new cast, became *Forever Knight. Forever Knight* was made possible by the proliferation of cable and UHF channels, while *Buffy the Vampire Slayer* has succeeded by becoming a centerpiece to the WB Network's targeting of the young female audience. Other television vampire series, such as ABC's weekly *The New Dark Shadows* and CBS's *Kindred* (based on the role-playing game "Masquerade," it deals with vampire clans who, like warring Mafia families, struggle for control of San Francisco), failed perhaps because they were marketed by older networks that wouldn't cultivate such a specific audience. The networks canceled *The New Dark Shadows* after thirteen episodes; *Kindred,* after six. Whether they might have succeeded in different time slots and with more support is a moot point, but it seems clear that these networks wanted a larger audience than they were able to get and were unwilling to cultivate such a one as WB has for *Buffy.* They may have also miscalculated in making their vampire protagonists romantic figures.

12. The series underwent major changes in the third season; Janette leaves Toronto, Schanke is killed in a plane crash, and Nick gets a new partner, Tracy Vetter, a young woman struggling with her role as a cop in the department where her father was commissioner. The new vampires Vachon and Urse also appear. Apparently, the world of vampires and humans was simply going to get more and more complex, but this also meant that the series lost focus, as Tracy became almost as central as Nick. Tracy knows Vachon is a vampire but never knows about

Nick. The youthful Tracy, Vachon (a sort of slacker vampire), and Urse (a suicidal, self-hating vampire) were likely meant to give the series more appeal to younger viewers. At the same time, episodes were often more didactic, losing the edge of ambiguity that characterized much of the first two seasons.

BIBLIOGRAPHY

Critical Works

Altner, Patricia. *Vampire Readings: An Annotated Bibliography.* Metuchen, N.J., 1998.

Auerbach, Nina. *Our Vampires, Ourselves.* Chicago: The University of Chicago Press, 1995.

Brunson, Matthew. *The Vampire Encyclopedia.* New York: Crown, 1993.

Copper, Basil. *The Vampire in Legend, Fact, and Art.* New York: Robert Hale, 1972.

Davison, Carol Margaret, and Paul Simpson-Howley. *Bram Stoker's Dracula: Sucking through the Century 1897–1997.* Toronto: Dundurn Press, 1997.

Dresser, Noreen. *American Vampires.* New York: Vintage, 1989.

Frayling, Christopher, ed. *Vampyres.* London: Faber and Faber, 1991.

Gorden, Joan, and Veronica Hollinger. *Blood Read: The Vampire as Metaphor in Contemporary Culture.* Philadelphia: University of Pennsylvania Press, 1997.

Haworth-Maden, Clare. *The Essential Dracula.* New York: Crescent, 1992.

Heldreth, Leonard G., and Mary Phar. *The Blood Is the Life: Vampires in Literature.* Bowling Green, Ohio: Popular Press, 1999.

Holte, James Craig. *Dracula in the Dark.* Westport, Conn.: Greenwood, 1998.

Hoppenstand, Gary, and Ray Browne, eds. *The Gothic World of Anne Rice.* Bowling Green, Ohio: Bowling Green State University Popular Press, 1996.

Hort, Barbara E. *Unholy Hungers: Encountering the Psychic Vampire in Ourselves and Others.* Boston: Shambala, 1996.

Hunter, Jack, ed. *House of Horror: The Complete Hammer Films Story.* London: Creation Books, 1973.

Hutchings, Peter. *Hammer and Beyond: The British Horror Film.* Manchester: Manchester University Press, 1993.

Leatherdale, Clive. *Dracula: The Novel and the Legend.* Rev. ed. Brighton: Desert Island Books, 1993.

Bibliography

Leatherdale, Clive. *The Origins of Dracula*. Reprint, Westcliff-on-Sea, United Kingdom: Desert Island Books, 1995.

MacDonald, D.L. *Poor Polidori: A Critical Biography of the Author of "The Vampyre."* Toronto: University of Toronto Press, 1995.

MacNally, Raymond, and Radu Florescu. *In Search of Dracula* Rev. ed. New York: Houghton Mifflin, 1992.

Marcus, Jana. *In the Shadow of the Vampire: Reflections from the World of Anne Rice.* New York: Thunder's Mouth Press, 1997.

Mascetti, Manuela Dunn. *Vampire: The Complete Guide to the World of the Undead.* New York: Viking Penguin, 1992.

Melton, J. Gordon. *The Vampire Book: The Encyclopedia of the Undead.* 2nd ed. Detroit: Visible Ink, 1999.

Miller, Elizabeth, ed. *Dracula: The Shade and the Shadow.* Westcliff-on-Sea, United Kingdom: Desert Island Books, 1998.

Page, Carol. *Bloodlust: Conversations with Real Vampires.* New York: Harper Collins, 1991.

Pirie, David. *A Heritage of Horror.* London: Gordon Fraiser, 1973.

Pirie, David. *Vampire Cinema.* New York: Crescent, 1977.

Ramsland, Katherine. *Prism in the Night: A Biography of Anne Rice.* New York: Dutton, 1991.

Ramsland, Katherine. *The Vampire Companion: The Official Guide to Anne Rice's* The Vampire Chronicles. New York: Ballantine, 1993.

Ramsland, Katherine. *Piercing the Darkness: Undercover with Vampires in America Today.* New York: Harper Collins, 1998.

Rickels, Laurence A. *The Vampire Lectures.* Minneapolis: University of Minnesota Press, 1999.

Ronay, Gabriel. *The Truth About Dracula.* London: Stein and Day, 1973.

Scott, Kathryn Leigh, ed. *The Dark Shadows Companion.* Los Angeles: Pomegranate Press, 1990.

Senf, Carol. *Dracula: Between Tradition and Modernism.* New York: Twayne Publishers, 1998.

Silver, Alain, and James Ursini. *The Vampire Film.* Rev. ed. New York: Limelight Editions, 1993.

Skal, David J. *Hollywood Gothic: The Tangled Web of Dracula from Stage to Screen.* New York: W.W. Norton, 1990.

Skal, David J. *V is for Vampire.* New York: Plume Penguin, 1996.

Twitchell, James B. *The Living Dead: A Study of the Vampire in Romantic Literature.* Durham: Duke University Press, 1981.

Waller, Gregory. *The Living and the Undead.* Urbana and Chicago: University of Illinois Press, 1986.

Wolf, Leonard. *The Essential Dracula.* New York: Broadway Books, 1997.

Bibliography

Vampire Stories: Print, Film, Television

Anthologies

Brite, Poppy Z., ed. *Love in Vein*. New York: Harper Prism, 1994.

Dalby, Richard, ed. *Dracula's Brood*. New York: Dorset Press, 1987.

Elrod, P.N., and Martin Greenberg, eds. *The Time of the Vampires*. New York: Daw Books, 1996.

Greenberg, Martin, ed. *Celebrity Vampires*. New York: Daw Books, 1995.

Greenberg, Martin, ed. *Vampire Detectives*. New York: Daw Books, 1995.

Haining, Peter, ed. *The Vampire Hunter's Casebook*. New York: Barnes and Noble, 1997.

Jones, Stephan, ed. *The Mammoth Book of Dracula*. New York: Carroll and Graf, 1997.

McCammon, Robert, ed. *Under the Fang*. New York: Pocket Books, 1991.

Ryan, Alan, ed. *Vampyres: Two Centuries of Great Vampire Stories*. Garden City: Doubleday & Co., 1987.

Stephens, John Richard, ed. *Vampires, Wine, and Roses*. New York: Berkeley Books, 1997.

Weinberg, Martin, Stefan Dziemianowicz, Martin Greenberg, eds. *100 Vicious Little Vampire Stories*. New York: Barnes and Noble, 1995.

———, eds. *Rivals of Dracula*. New York: Barnes and Noble, 1996.

Zweifel, Karyn. *Southern Vampires*. Birmingham: Crane Hill Publishers, 1996.

Novels

Anscombe, Roderick. *The Secret Life of Lazlo, Count Dracula*. New York: Hyperion, 1994.

Charnas, Suzy McKee. *The Vampire Tapestry*. New York: Simon and Schuster, 1981.

Collins, Nancy. *Midnight Blue: The Sonja Blue Collection*. Stone Mountain: White Wolf Press, 1995. Reprint compiling the novels originally published as *Sunglasses after Dark* (1992), *In the Blood* (1993), and *Paint It Black* (1994).

Elrod, P.N. *Bloodlist*. New York: Ace Books, 1990.

——— *Lifeblood*. New York: Ace Books, 1990.

——— *Bloodcircle*. New York: Ace Books, 1990.

——— *Art in the Blood*. New York: Ace Books, 1991.

——— *Fire in the Blood*. New York: Ace Books, 1991.

——— *Blood in the Water*. New York: Ace Books, 1992.

——— *A Chill in the Blood*. New York: Ace Books, 1998.

——— *The Dark Sleep*. New York: Ace Books, 1999.

——— *Lady Crymsyn*. New York: Ace Books, 2000.

Gomez, Jewelle. *The Gilda Stories*. Ithaca: Firebrand Books, 1991.

Holland, Tom. *Lord of the Dead*. New York: Simon and Schuster, 1995.

Kilpatrick, Nancy. *Child of the Night*. Nottingham, United Kingdom: Pumpkin Books, 1996.

King, Stephen. *'Salem's Lot*. New York: Doubleday, 1976.

Bibliography

Kiraly, Marie. *Mina*. New York: Berkley Pub. Group, 1994.

LeFanu, Sheridan. *Carmilla*. n.p., 1872.

Martin, George R.R. *Fevre Dream*. New York: Doubleday & Co., 1982.

Newman, Kim. *Anno Dracula*. New York: Carroll and Graf, 1992.

———. *The Bloody Red Baron*. New York: Carroll and Graf, 1995.

———. *Judgment of Tears: Anno Dracula 1959*. New York: Carroll and Graf, 1998.

Pike, Christopher. *The Last Vampire*. New York: Pocket Books, 1994.

Rice, Anne. *Interview with the Vampire*. New York: Alfred A. Knopf, 1976.

———. *The Vampire Lestat*. New York: Alfred A. Knopf, 1985.

———. *The Queen of the Damned*. New York: Alfred A. Knopf, 1988.

Romkey, Michael. *I, Vampire*. New York: Ballantine, 1990.

———. *The Vampire Papers*. New York: Ballantine, 1994.

———. *Vampire Princess*. New York: Ballantine, 1996.

Rymer, James Malcolm. *Varney the Vampire; or The Feast of Blood*. London: F. Lloyd, 1847. Reprint, ed. E.F. Blieler, New York: Dover, 1972. Reprint, ed. Devendra P. Varma, New York: Arno Press, 1970.

Sabgerhagen, Fred. *The Dracula Tape*. New York: Warner, 1975.

Simmons, Dan. *Children of the Night*. New York: G.P. Putnam, 1992.

Steakley, John. *Vampire$*. New York: Penguin, 1990.

Stoker, Bram. *Dracula*. 1896.

———. *Dracula: A Norton Critical Edition*. ed. Nina Auerbach and David Skal. New York: W.W. Norton & Co., 1997.

Strieber, Whitley. *The Hunger*. New York: William Morrow & Co., 1981.

Yarbro, Chelsea Quinn. *Hotel Transylvania*. New York: St. Martin's Press, 1978.

———. *The Palace*. New York: St. Martin's Press, 1978.

———. *Blood Games*. New York: St. Martin's Press, 1981.

———. *Path of the Eclipse*. New York: St. Martin's Press, 1981.

———. *Tempting Fate*. New York: St. Martin's Press, 1982.

———. *The Saint-Germian Chronicles*. New York: Simon and Schuster, 1983.

———. *Darker Jewels*. New York: Tor, 1992.

———. *Out of the House of Life*. New York: Tor, 1994.

———. *Mansions of Darkness*. New York: Tor, 1996.

———. *Writ in Blood*. New York: Tor, 1997.

———. *Blood Roses*. New York: Tor, 1998.

———. *Communion Blood*. New York: Tor, 1999.

———. *Come Twilight*. New York: Tor, 2000.

Film

The Addiction. Dir. Abel Ferrera. October Films, 1995.

Blacula. Dir. William Crain. American International Pictures, 1972.

Blood for Dracula. Dir. Paul Morrissey and (uncredited) Anthony Dawson. CC Champion/Jean Yanne–Jean Pierre Rassam/Warhol Productions, 1993.

Bram Stoker's Dracula. Dir. Francis Ford Coppola. Columbia/Zoetrope/Osiris, 1992.

Def By Temptation. Dir. James Bond III. Orpheus/Bonded Filmworks/Troma, 1990.

Bibliography

Dracula. Dir. Tod Browning. Universal, 1931.
Dracula. Dir. John Badham. Mirisch/UA, 1979.
Dracula 2000. Dir. Patrick Lussier. Dimension Films, 2000.
Dracula Has Risen from the Grave. Dir. Freddie Francis. Hammer Films, 1968.
Dracula, Prince of Darkness. Dir. Terence Fisher. Hammer Films/SevenArts, 1966.
Fright Night. Dir. Tom Holland. Columbia, 1985.
Fright Night, Part 2. Dir. Tommy Lee Wallace. Tristar/Vista, 1988.
Habit. Dir. Larry Fessenden. Glass Eye Pix, 1997.
Horror of Dracula. Dir. Terence Fisher. Hammer Films, 1958.
House of Dark Shadows. Dir. Dan Curtis. MGM, 1971.
The Hunger. Dir. Tony Scott. MGM, 1983.
Kiss of the Vampire. Dir. Don Sharp. Hammer Films, 1964.
The Lost Boys. Dir. Joel Schumacher. Warner Brothers, 1987.
Love at First Bite. Dir. Stan Dragoti. Simon Productions/American International Pictures, 1979.
Lust for a Vampire. Dir. Jimmy Sangster. Hammer Films, 1971.
Martin. Dir. George Romero. Braddock Associates/Libra/Laurel Group, 1976.
Najda. Dir. Michael Almeredya. October Films, 1994.
Near Dark. Dir. Kathryn Bigelow. DEG/Feldman-Meeker, 1987.
Nosferatu. Dir. F.W. Murnau. Prana Films, 1922.
Nosferatu. Dir. Werner Herzog. Herzog/Gaumont, 1979.
Once Bitten. Dir. Howard Storm. Goldwyn, 1985.
Scars of Dracula. Dir. Roy Ward Baker. Hammer Films, 1970.
Scream, Blacula, Scream. Dir. Bob Kelljan. American International Pictures, 1973.
Shadow of the Vampire. Dir. E. Elias Merhige. British Broadcasting Company, 2000.
Sundown: the Vampire in Retreat. Dir. Anthony Hickox. Verston, 1990.
Taste the Blood of Dracula. Dir. Peter Sadasy. Hammer Films, 1970.
Twins of Evil. Dir. John Hough. Hammer Films, 1971.
Vampire Lovers. Dir. Roy Ward Baker. Hammer Films/American International Pictures, 1970.
Vampire's Kiss. Dir. Robert Bierman. Hemdale, 1989.
Vampyr. Dir. Carl Dryer. Tobia-Klangfilm, 1932.
Vamp. Dir. Richard Wenk. New World/Balcor, 1986.

Television
Buffy the Vampire Slayer. Kuzui Productions, 1997–present.
Dark Shadows. Dan Curtis Productions, 1966–1971.
Dracula. Dan Curtis Productions, 1974.
Forever Knight. Pargon Productions, 1992–1995.
Kindred: The Embraced. Aaron Spelling Productions, 1996.
The Night Stalker. Dan Curtis Productions, 1972.
Vampire. ABC/MTM, 1979.

INDEX

Index

Index

191

Index